P!NK GOLDF!SH 2.0

DEFY NORMAL AND EXPLOIT IMPERFECTION

STAN PHELPS
&
DAVID RENDALL

Published by 9 INCH Marketing

Layout by Amit Dey, Cover Design by Josh Vaughan of Blue Barn Design Co., Cover Photography by Kevin Seifert of RTP Studio, and Indexing by Faye Bulawin

ISBN: 978-1-952234-11-8

First Printing: 2021

Printed in the United States of America

P!NK GOLDF!SH 2.0 is available for bulk orders. For further details and special pricing, please email stan@purplegoldfish.com or dave@drendall.com.

DEDICATION

This book is dedicated to my youngest son, James Phelps.
Your weaknesses hold the keys to your strengths.
Never stop embracing what makes you unique and special.

—Stan Phelps

This book is dedicated to my parents, Vernon and Shary,
and my grandparents, Leland and Ruby.

—David Rendall

ACKNOWLEDGMENTS

We'd like to thank everyone who inspired us, supported us, or provided feedback for *PINK GOLDFISH* and *P!NK GOLDF!SH 2.0*:

Arif Abdulla, Karen Albritton, Jamie Anderson, Matt Anderson, Kenneth Anum, Jay Baer, Ben Baker, Ben Baldanza, Marilynn Barber, Brent Barbour, Andrew Barton, Brady Bell, Jeff Bezos, Josh Bledsoe, Laszlo Bock, Alex Bogusky, Jake Bohall, Richard Branson, Troyen A. Brennan, Martyn Brewer, Jared Brickman, Faye Bulawin, Bo Burlingham, Skip Carney, Evan Carroll, S. Truett Cathy, Dorie Clark, Marty Cobb, Steve Cody, Josh Coffy, Ben Cohen, Sandy Colon, Scott Cook, Julian Cromer, Ted Curtin, Trisha Cuzdey, Elisa Daalder, Dietmar Dahman, Ray Dalio, Alec Dalton, Kironmoy Datta, Adam DeSantis, Dennis Devlin, Minter Dial, Brian Doyle, Frank Druffel, Scott Dudley, Johnny Earle, Bryan Elanko, Karen Eugenio, Jason Falls, Robert Ferguson, Veronica (Niki) Fielding, John Fluevog, Michael Franken, Christopher Fuller, Phil Gerbyshak, Earlene Gibbons, Lance Gibbs, Stacey Gipson, Greg Glassman, Cody Goldberg, WL Gore, Keith Green, David Guerra, Sean-Michael Green, Lewis Greenberg, Shaun Griffith, Chris Guillebeau, David Hadden, Chad Hahn, Darren Hamilton, Steven Handmaker, Phil Hansen, Chip Heath, Dan Heath, Lee Heinrich, Keith Herrmann, Michelle Hill, Michael Hobbs, Gregg Hook, Tony Hsieh, Jackie Huba, Jony Ive, Rick Jarrett, Steve Jobs, Emily Juhnke, Shawn Kanungo, Max Kampenaar, Russ Klein, Ashley Knepper, Takeru Kobayashi, Kristin Kohler Burrows, Azhar Laher, Lazarus Lake, Judy Lahner, Joseph Lalonde, Jim Lawenda, Tim League, Michelle LeBlanc, Adriana Lee, Tammy Lenski, Rick Liebling, Lisa Lindstrom, John Mackey, R. Mark Macy, Mike Maddock, Elizabeth Magill, Chris Malone, Mireille Masue, Sharon Delaney McCloud, Madi McDougald, Lauren McGhee, Dr. Gary McGrath, Steve McDonald, Suzanne Miglucci, Gary Mintchell, Rebecca Minkoff, Michelle Miracle, Youngme Moon, Jerry Murrell, Sumner Musolf, Drew Neisser, Martha O'Gorman, Michael O'Leary, Theresa Pantazopoulos, Chris Parker, Tom Peters, Jennifer Phelps, Tim Phelps, Dan Pink, Jeff Pocklington, Keeley Pomeroy, Praveen Puri, Andy Puzder, Anna Rendall, Emma Rendall, Sophia Rendall, Stephanie Rendall, Cory Richardson, Richard Riche, Danny Rosin, Allen Roy, Lisa Ryan, Karl Sakas, Paige Sandhu, Emily Sander, Victoria Sanders, Mark Sanna, Kimberly Schubeck, Vince Schmidt, Kevin Seifert, Bhupesh Shah, Herbert Sherman, Brittany Silva, Spencer Silver, Mary Sikorski, Jeff Sommers, Earl Springer, LeAnn Stephenson, Melissa St. John, Tiffany Sturdivant, Rajan Tata, Beth Thuin, Deanne Topping, Lynsi Torres, Joshua Vaughan, Jimmy Vee, Mark Villalovos, Melanie Vracas, Becky Vucksta, Ruth Graves Wakefield, Red Wassenich, Jeremy Watkin, Alyssa Waxenberg, Joe Webb, Jenn Wheeler, Norm Wood, Hayley Woodin, and Misty Young.

PRAISE FOR
P!NK GOLDF!SH 2.0

"Don't hide the weird and the wacky parts of your organization. Use them to stand out from the crowd. Forget about strengths (or set them to the side for a minute). Leverage your weaknesses into the unique qualities that set you apart. These are the core messages of this smart book... Think about it. All the other goldfish are, well, gold. Imagine how you might thrive as the only pink goldfish in the pond."

— Daniel Pink,
author of *WHEN* and *DRIVE*

"Packed with incredible examples, this book will have you spotting Pink Goldfish everywhere, and inspire you to breed your own, ASAP!"

— Jay Baer
founder of Convince & Convert and author of *Talk Triggers*

"Pink Goldfish offers a smart, powerful, and vibrant framework for any company that wants to stand out. Filled with fascinating case studies, this book shows how businesses can turn perceived flaws into strengths and connect authentically with their customers."

— Dorie Clark,
author of *Reinventing You* and *Stand Out*

CONTENTS

FOREWORD

Today, word of mouth is the most effective and least expensive way to gain new customers.

This was also true five years ago. It has always been true. It was true when the first caveman sold a better-than-expected arrowhead to another caveman. It will always be true.

Yet, very, very, VERY few businesses make any meaningful attempt to boost word of mouth. Instead, it's just taken for granted. It is nearly always assumed that if the organization just does a good job, and executes well, customers will naturally notice that excellence, and tell others about it. This is what most company leaders think.

But each of those leaders is expecting customers to behave how they themselves do not. Because the fact is that all human beings ignore what is average, and discuss what is different.

Competency doesn't create conversation. It never has, and it never will.

Competency keeps customers from defecting. But it doesn't create new customers. Why? Because we EXPECT competency. That's what we're paying for, after all. And we don't make a point of telling our friends about that time we got exactly what we expected. This is why there are so few 3-star reviews: "Paid for a sandwich. Got a sandwich. 3 stars." If there is no story to tell, we simply don't tell it.

I have had six accountants in my professional career. All of them are competent, as far as I can tell. Yet, I have quite literally never told a story about any of them, to anyone. What would be the gist of that tale? "You won't believe it! I got my tax return back, and all of the numbers added up!"

To turn your current customers into volunteer marketers on your behalf, you need more than competency: you need something different, and distinct, and memorable. If you want more stories told about you, you need to be worthy of a story.

P!NK GOLDF!SH 2.0 is your instruction manual for unlocking and implementing your uniqueness, which becomes the plot line for those stories.

I have spent nearly 30 years as a marketing and customer experience advisor to major brands, and have written or co-written six books in the category. I have had the pleasure of knowing Stan

Phelps and David Rendall for many of those years. I love their work throughout the Goldfish series, but *P!NK GOLDF!SH 2.0* is closest to my heart.

Why?

Because after consulting with more than 700 organizations, I have found it to be exceedingly difficult to find lasting success in business without meaningful differentiation. If you're disproportionately good at marketing, that will help. If you're better than average at customer service, that will help. If you have - at least temporarily - a product that is actually superior, that will help. If you have exceedingly devoted employees, that will help.

But none of these is enough to create significant, sustained success.

You have to stand out in a way that is noticeable enough to create a tsunami of stories about that differentiator.

In short: if you're not a Pink Goldfish, eventually you'll become a sick goldfish.

Being different is critical, yet few organizations choose to actually be different. Why?

For my book about word of mouth, I studied why organizations fail to embrace different, and found there are three main hurdles:

1. Leaders don't understand why differentiation is needed

2. Leaders don't understand how to differentiate, or in what way

3. Leaders don't have the courage to differentiate (if it ain't broke, don't fix it)

What I love most about *P!NK GOLDF!SH 2.0* is that it addresses all three of these obstacles. This book makes a sturdy case for why different matters. This book - with its sublime FLAWSOME system - shows you precisely all the ways different can work. And this book illustrates why different should be embraced, not shunned.

Further, it's common in marketing and customer experience books to be presented with some case studies and examples that are a bit too tidy: they are shoehorned and gerrymandered to perfectly fit the narrative, but leave the reader not sure how to apply the principles in their own situation. This is not that book.

Indeed, the number of stories, and ideas, and inspirational detective work contained in these pages is extraordinary. You will find a cornucopia of examples in this book that make you think, "you know, if we put a twist on that, it could work for us." If you don't, you're just being obstinate.

I know you will enjoy *P!NK GOLDF!SH 2.0.* It's an engaging and exciting read. It's the kind of book you tell your boss about when you're half-way through. And if you're the boss, it's the kind of book you call a team meeting about when you're half-way through.

But don't start yet. Be prepared first. You will be propelled by the ideas and the humor and the overall accessibility of this work. You will not want to stop, so make sure you're not trying to start reading this book in a 15-minute gap between your next appointment.

First, clear your calendar.

Then, clear your mind.

Now you're ready for the Pink Goldfish.

Enjoy!

Jay Baer
Founder of Convince & Convert
Co-author of *Talk Triggers: The Complete Guide to Creating Customers with Word of Mouth*

INTRODUCTION

BY

DAVID RENDALL & STAN PHELPS

*The search for meaningful distinction
is central to the marketing effort.
If marketing is about anything,
it is about achieving customer-getting distinction
by differentiating what you do and how you operate.
All else is derivative of that and only that.*

— Theodore Levitt, economist and professor

I (David) was walking through Target with my daughters and a children's book caught my attention. This is important because my girls are teenagers and they don't read children's books anymore. I wasn't even looking for books and I certainly wasn't looking for an illustrated book for kids. The book wasn't relevant to me personally, but I still noticed it.

The title was *P is for Pterodactyl*. I saw it out of the corner of my eye and kept walking. But then I started thinking about that title. Pterodactyl isn't a very good word to use if the goal is to teach kids what the letter P sounds like. In fact, it's a terrible word to use as an example. Why would someone do that? What a dumb book idea.

I had to turn around and go back. I needed more information. This is what I saw on the cover.

P is for Pterodactyl

- The Worst Alphabet Book Ever
- All the letters that misbehave and make words nearly impossible to pronounce

But why? Why would you write a bad book on purpose? Isn't the goal to write a good book, a better book, or the best book? For most people, it is. Most books are supposed to be good books. Their author tries to do a good job, maybe even a great job, writing the book.

That is why *P is for Pterodactyl* got my attention, got me thinking, got me to stop, turned me around, and got me to take a second look. Once I took a second look, I wanted to know more. I did a *Google* search when I got home. I read the *Wikipedia* page. I looked inside the book on *Amazon*. I immediately added the book to my Pink Goldfish keynote presentation and shared it with 1,000 conference attendees in Phoenix, Arizona.

The book was bad on purpose and that made it more interesting than all of the other alphabet books that are essentially the same. They all do a good job teaching kids about the sounds that letters make. But, if you're going to write a new alphabet book, and you hope to sell copies and make money, how would you make your book stand out? How would you differentiate it from all the others? Instead of trying to write a better book, write a worse book, on purpose.

Would that work? Absolutely.

P is for Pterodactyl was written by a rapper, Raj Haldar (aka Lushlife). It is currently the #1 search result on *Amazon.com* for alphabet books for children. It was still ranked #791 in all books on *Amazon.com* more than two years after publication. The first printing of 10,800 copies sold out on the first day, and over 200,000 have been sold to date. 10,000 is the industry standard for a successful book. The book also has almost 6,500 reviews with an average rating of 4.8 out of 5, and it was a *New York Times* #1 bestseller for children's picture books on December 30, 2018, just over a month after publication.

On October 19, 2018, Maria Russo featured *P is for Pterodactyl* in an article in the *New York Times*.[1] She said, "you can curse the English language for its insane spelling rules (or lack thereof), or you can delight in it, as this raucous trip through the odd corners of our alphabet does." Haldar is *unapologetic* about how bad his book is. He parades it without shame, and he also *flaunts* the weaknesses of the English language. He doesn't try to hide them, he *exposes* them.

And this isn't an isolated case . . .

Think about what you expect in a book for children. The first thing that comes to mind is pictures. Children's books win awards for illustrations. Illustration is a profession. You can't write a book for kids if it doesn't have pictures, but that's exactly what B.J. Novak did.

Novak is a producer, actor, writer, and director of the hit television show *The Office*. He is also the author of *The Book with No Pictures*, which was published in September 2014. Novak could have found an illustrator. He could have hired one of the best illustrators in the world, but he didn't. He deliberately wrote a book for children with no pictures. We call this *opposing*, doing the opposite of what everyone else in a category or industry is doing.

Did it work? Definitely.

Critics loved it. Mark Levine from the *New York Times* said that the book is "conceptually radical... making the refreshing and contrarian case that words alone have sensory and imaginative vibrancy to spare." *Bustle.com* said that it is "unlike any of the children's books you read growing up."

Parents and children loved it. *The Book with No Pictures* has over 12,000 reviews on *Amazon.com* with an average rating of 4.8 out of 5. It is still ranked #448 in all books on *Amazon.com*, seven years after it was released.

But, to be clear, not everyone loved these two unique books.

P is for Pterodactyl has 65 one-star reviews on *Amazon.com*. Some people are upset because the book references a Ouija board for the letter O. One of those reviews is ominously titled, "evil lurking."

---

1. https://www.nytimes.com/2018/10/19/books/review/parade-of-elephants-kevin-henkes.html

Other reviewers are clearly educators and they criticize the book for not being an effective learning tool. It seems like they might have misunderstood the point of the book.

Similarly, *The Book with No Pictures* has more than 125 one-star reviews on Amazon.com. Some of them are mean and personal. "Don't waste your money. . . If Ryan Howard were a book: Unfunny & Shallow." Others call the book "stupid. . . not funny. . . dumb. . . useless. . . disappointing. . . not interesting. . . terrible. . . uneducated meaningless junk."

As successful as both of these books are, they aren't universally loved. In fact, some people really hate them. We call this Antagonizing. Your efforts to differentiate are going to rub some people the wrong way.

In other words, not everyone thinks weird is wonderful. We discovered that when we asked for feedback on new cover designs for *P!NK GOLDF!SH 2.0*.

Photo Credit: Stan Phelps

Some people rejected all of the options. They were unimpressed by our strange nonsense and they spent a surprising amount of time telling us what we were doing wrong. Here's some of the feedback:

- All of these are very difficult to read. They may grab the eye with their garish colors, but they are all illegible. Whatever happened to "form follows function?" I would not buy this book solely based on the cover. Hideous.

- Honestly none. Nothing wrong with being flashy, but these are borderline illegible. Drop the upside-down and reverse text.

- Sadly, none. You're asking too much of the reader. If I can't get it all in a matter of seconds, I'm on to the next title. Sorry. Remember the power of white space!

- I cannot tell what the tone of the book is. Is it calm? Considered? Frenetic? Angry? Fiction? Non-fiction? Self-help? Let alone get an inkling of the topic, which is the most essential purpose of a jacket. I cannot read the title, let alone the taglines. I really do not know what the book is about. I'm sorry. You asked for opinions. As a successful publisher said, stay away from pinks and purples, especially intense tones and hues!

- Good luck with a new design. Sometimes it's best to start again.

- It seems like you are trying to be different just to be different. Yes. I understand about exploiting imperfection, and you're trying to show that, but not on the book cover. I'd get annoyed by having to keep turning the book upside down to read the cover and I'd put it back on the shelf. And is it an eBook too? If so, you can't turn your computer upside-down to read stuff.

Additionally, the votes were very polarizing. Dave's favorite was B, but it did not get the most votes. In fact, it got a lot of anti-votes. Some people didn't just vote *for* A or C, they also voted *against* B. They told us *not* to use it. Here is the negative feedback for B:

- Not B. *Too crowded* and the text is disorienting

- *Too busy*
- B is *too busy*
- B is far *too busy*
- B is *too busy* and overwhelming
- B is a little *too busy* for my eyes

- B is *too much*
- B is just *too much*

- I just find it *too much*

- *Too much.* I had to *look* away

- B is *too much* and I didn't want to even *look* at it

- I want to *look* away from B because it is *too much* to digest

- B is *too crazy*, makes me anxious

- B is hard to read

- It's just *too hard* to tell what it's about

- Illegible

- Cluttered

- B accosts

- Demands attention, but the eye doesn't know where to go

- May be disruptive and antagonistic, which is what you are going for, but not at the expense of readability

B got the least number of votes and was the only one that people actively disliked, but it wasn't universally hated. A minority of responders really liked B. Here are some of their comments:

- I like B. Nice and *bold!*

- I love the *boldness* of B

- B. Fortune favors the *bold.*

- B is the *boldest!* It really stands out to me.

- I would prefer B. Looks fresh and *bold!* But hey, content first :-)

- Me Agrada El B. (translation: I Like B)

- I do like B

- I like B. It highlights pink more than the other covers.

- B. For eating your own dog food

- B. Because it covers the full page

- B. It makes you stop to look and see what it says

- B is more eye-catching in my opinion

- B. The text gives the illusion there is more

- Something is drawing me to B. Perhaps because it stands out from the others ;-)

Here are the final results of the voting:

A - 55%
C - 35%
B - 10%

So what did we do? Well, after counting the votes, we did the *opposite* of what most authors and publishers would have done. We chose the cover that people liked the least, and we rejected the covers that they liked the most. We chose B, which was liked by just 10 percent of voters, and rejected A, which was liked by 55 percent of voters, and rejected C, which was liked by 35 percent of voters. We deliberately chose the worst cover. We did it wrong on purpose.

Now, I know what you're thinking. What does this have to do with you? You're not trying to write a bestselling children's book or design a cover for the second edition of a moderately successful business book. You're trying to run an effective business. How do the lessons from these odd books apply to marketing and strategy for companies and organizations?

Those are the questions we hope to answer in the following pages. Unusual children's books and our weird book cover are great illustrations of Pink Goldfish, and they're just a few of over 350 company, product, and personal branding examples we've researched. Buckle up, there are many more to come. Stan and I have been collecting them for quite a while…

Now, let's have Stan share a bit of background on the Goldfish Series.

SEARCHING FOR DIFFERENTIATION

I (Stan) began my writing in 2008 with a blog called 9 INCH marketing. Nothing personal unfortunately. Those nine inches (23 centimeters) are a reference to the average distance between the stem of your brain and the top of your heart. The journey from the brain to the heart of your customer is the longest and hardest nine inches in all of marketing. Over the course of that first year, I blogged about 50 different marketing-related topics.

I was searching for what I thought would be a game-changer in marketing and business. In 2009, I experienced a "moment of truth" in New York City that changed my life and focus.

It was a summer evening, and I was with a work colleague. Brad and I were at a trendy New York rooftop bar. One of those places in Manhattan where a bottle of beer is 15 bucks. We were waiting to meet a few people before heading over to a networking event. I noticed an older gentleman sitting on his own across from us. As the minutes passed, it became obvious that he was waiting for someone. After half an hour passed, I decided to strike up a conversation.

I leaned in and jokingly asked the man, "Do you know that we spend 10 percent of our life waiting?" I assured him I knew this was true because I once had read it on the internet. We laughed and then started talking about the etiquette of waiting. I stressed the importance of being on time. Right then the old man shook his head and said something I'll never forget.

"There is no such thing as being on time. In fact, being on time is a myth," he said. Wait a second, I thought. I've been on time before. He waved his finger at me Dikembe Mutombo style and asserted, "No. Being on time is a fallacy. In life, you are either early...or you are late. No one is ever on time."

This was a complete paradigm shift for me. I went home that night and started thinking about how this applies to business. My mind immediately linked this to marketing and meeting customer expectations. I've always thought that the idea of simply meeting expectations was a surefire recipe for disaster. It almost guarantees you will fall short.

I walked away from that brief conversation with a new conviction. Too much attention was being placed on awareness and acquisition in marketing. I believed that successful businesses would need to find the "little things" to maximize the customer experience by putting customers first; taking care of the customers they had, in other words, so those customers would bring them the (referred) customers they wanted.

I became a disciple of the late Theodore Levitt, a former Harvard Business School professor, who believed that businesses should put the customer at the center of everything they do. Levitt asserted, "The search for meaningful distinction is central to the marketing effort. If marketing is about anything, it is about achieving customer-getting distinction by differentiating what you do and how you operate. All else is derivative of that and only that."

I believed the focus of business should be on customers and not just chasing the bottom-line. Profit was the result, not the aim. I believed experience was the route to competitive differentiation and would soon become the new marketing. *P!NK GOLDF!SH 2.0* focuses on customer-getting distinction via differentiation.

MEETING DAVID

I met my co-author (David) at a networking event hosted by Dr. Kevin C. Snyder back in 2013. David was hard to miss in the room. Beyond his 6'6" height, David was wearing pink pants and pink sneakers. That night I learned about *The Freak Factor*. This seminal book outlines a simple premise—what makes us weird can make us wonderful and what makes us weak can also make us strong.

In the words of acclaimed author Daniel Pink, "David Rendall has a radical prescription for chronic dissatisfaction: Stop working on your weaknesses and start amplifying them instead. *The Freak Factor* flips the cult of self-improvement on its head with stories of real people who have soared to success by embracing their uniqueness."

The principles in *The Freak Factor* have universal application. They can be applied to personal development, leadership, parenting, and relationships. I immediately saw the power of the principles and how they applied to business strategy and marketing. We would partner up in 2016 and work together to launch the original *Pink Goldfish* in 2018.

THE KEY TO LIFE AND HUMOR IS...

The key to life and humor is ... timing. David and I have purposely decided to launch the update to our original book on July 5, 2021.

Why? Because July 4th is a defining date for the COVID-19 pandemic.

President Biden shared in April 2021, "This is our target date to get life in America closer to normal and begin to celebrate our independence from the virus together with our friends and our loved ones as we celebrate Independence Day."

July 5th will begin Day 2 of life after COVID. What should we call this "After-Corona" time?

> A. THE NEXT NORMAL
> B. THE NEW NORMAL
> C. THE NO NORMAL

We think it should be C. If the global pandemic has done anything, it has taught us that all of our norms need to be challenged. We have to question everything.

Credit goes to Alan Weiss for coining (and trademarking) NO NORMAL. In his words, "My concept of the immediate future is No Normal™. Not 'back to normal' or a 'new normal.' We're going to have to be agile and maneuverable and deal with ambiguity and turmoil continually. We need to use disruption and volatility as offensive weapons."[2]

Successful firms going forward will need to raise the bar, not restore it. *P!NK GOLDF!SH 2.0* uncovers how to do it.

---

2. https://alanweiss.com/no-normal

"We're living history, surprise after surprise after surprise. And just when we think we've had all the big surprises for a while, along comes another one. If the first two decades of the 21st century have taught us anything, it is that uncertainty is chronic; instability is permanent; disruption is common; and we can neither predict nor govern events. There will be no 'new normal.' There will only be a continuous series of 'not normal' episodes, defying prediction, and unforeseen by most of us until they happen."

— Jim Collins, from the book *Beyond Entrepreneurship 2.0*

COMPETING ON DIFFERENTIATION

In her book *Different - Escaping the Competitive Herd*, Harvard Business School marketing professor Youngme Moon argues that "the ability to compete is dependent upon the ability to differentiate from competitors." However, she goes on to say, "The number of companies who are truly able to achieve competitive separation is depressingly small." This is because companies tend to define their strengths and weaknesses using the same measurements and standards as their competitors. This leads to homogeneity, not differentiation. When everyone is trying to build on the same strengths and eliminate the same weaknesses, all companies start to look the same.

So, how can you create one of the few organizations that become extraordinary? How can you succeed where most organizations fail? The goal of *P!NK GOLDF!SH 2.0* is to help you to compete more effectively by becoming truly different.

This book is broken into three main sections:

Section I outlines the **Why**.

It explores the need to embrace weirdness and amplify weakness to differentiate in business. We reveal how everything we've learned about weakness is wrong. We show how every weakness has a corresponding strength. We examine the seven reasons to embrace weirdness. The section ends with an explanation of our metaphor of the Pink Goldfish. We'll share the symbolism of the goldfish and the reasoning behind the color pink.

Section II showcases the **What**.

Here we examine the concept of being F.L.A.W.S.O.M.E. This is the idea of embracing your flaws. You can succeed because of your flaws, not despite them. We use F.L.A.W.S.O.M.E. as our acronym for the eight types of Pink Goldfish. We share our flaunting matrix and each type: **F**launting,

Lopsiding, Antagonizing, Withholding, Swerving, Opposing, Micro-weirding, and Exposing. This section points out the ways to stand out by doing more of what makes you inherently imperfect, and intentionally less of what others consider normal and strong in business.

Section III explains the **How**.

Here we share the process of finding your own Pink Goldfish. We delve into the six A's. The first A is **A**ssess, and it involves understanding what makes you imperfect. The second A is **A**ppreciate. Appreciation is accepting and taking ownership of your uniqueness. The third A is **A**lign. Aligning is about finding those areas of weirdness and weakness that resonate with your customer and create meaningful differentiation. The fourth A is **A**mplifi. Amplification is the process of turning up or turning down the dial to bring your differentiation to life. The fifth A is **A**ugment. Augmenting is combining two or more strategies to become even more unique. The sixth and final A is **A**ttack. Attack will provide insight on how to exploit the weaknesses of your competition.

Ready to jump in? We'll start with a new perspective on organizational strengths and weaknesses. Let's go…

OVERVIEW (THE WHY)

CHAPTER 1

WHY WEAKNESS?

"We are led to truth by our weaknesses as well as our strengths."

— Parker Palmer

Everything we've learned about weakness and imperfection is wrong. It's good to be strong and it's bad to be weak. Right? Perfection is the goal. Imperfection needs to be corrected and avoided. Right? Maybe not.

Have you ever heard of HARU URARA? The name in Japanese means *Glorious Spring*. She was a racehorse, based in Kochi, with a major flaw. Haru had raced 88 times and never won, but the announcer at the track noticed that Haru Urara would still trot energetically to the track and give her all in races, despite her many losses.

It was 2003 and Japan was in the midst of a deep depression. It was so bad that the previous 10 years were known as the *Lost Decade* given the downturn. The situation was dire and the Kochi Racetrack was facing closure.

The demise of the track was imminent until a local reporter wrote about Haru's noble failure. The article by Ken Ishii caught fire and soon everyone was talking about the horse with Hello Kitty patches on her pink facemask. She became famous, not because of winning, but because of her failure, her weakness. Haru Uraru and her "never give up spirit" captured the heart of a nation.

The horse would remain flawed. Despite her dogged persistence, Haru would end her career with zero wins in 111 races. She became a symbol of never giving up and was embraced by the Japanese people. Her weakness was the source of her popularity. Maybe there's a lesson in her story for the rest of us.

David Rendall learned about the connection between weakness and strength in a very personal way. He explains his revelation in *The Freak Factor*:

> I spent my whole life getting in trouble because I couldn't sit still, be quiet, and do what I was told. Then at some point, as an adult, I realized I was getting paid to stand up, talk, and run my own business. The very thing that people spent their whole life telling me not to do (my own parents used to call me "motormouth") was the thing I was getting paid for. It was the thing that I was doing really well.
>
> I discovered that my weaknesses were strengths. I started to wonder whether that may be true for other people and in business. I developed the concept of the Freak Factor, developed an assessment, wrote a book, and started gathering stories about how seemingly obvious weaknesses are also strengths and how the things that sometimes we're fixing to get better are actually the things we should be flaunting or amplifying or embracing.

But this isn't what we are taught at home, school, and work. Our parents, teachers, and managers teach us that we need to find and fix our flaws in order to be successful in life and business. There are four elements to this seemingly universal belief system.

1. We believe that to be successful we need to be normal, fit in, and not stand out. This means that we should be strong and follow the herd.

2. We think we should fix weaknesses and improve flaws in our companies. We believe that well-rounded and well-balanced companies are the ones that win.

3. Third, we're convinced that our company could be great at everything if we are diligent enough. Similarly, we think we could make everyone, or at least most people, happy if we try hard enough.

4. We believe that our company could stand out if we just have the discipline and perseverance to be better than the competition.

All of these beliefs seem empowering, but they are actually debilitating. They tell us that we have the potential to succeed, but they mislead us as to where that potential lies and how we should apply that potential. These beliefs lead to companies defining their strengths and weaknesses using the same measurements and standards as their competitors.

This book shatters these misconceptions by offering four competing beliefs:

1. Fitting in and becoming a copycat brand will never lead to success. Benchmarking and best practices are not the path to greatness.

2. Trying to fix a weakness is a waste of time and effort.

3. If you try to be great at everything, you will end up being great at nothing. If you try to please everyone, you won't end up pleasing anyone. You'll end up average, mediocre, and invisible.

4. Discipline and perseverance are finite resources. We have to be efficient in how and when we choose to use them.

We believe that it is good to be different, to stick out, and be unique. We believe that it is good to flaunt your weaknesses, instead of fixing them. It is good to be unbalanced. We believe that the flaws of a brand can make it awesome, just like Haru Urara.

This may seem like a ridiculous argument. If you're skeptical, that's okay. You should be. We'll spend the rest of the book demonstrating the value of exploiting imperfection.

Before we do that, we found some interesting connections between weakness and the color pink that we want to share with you. This fascinating story is in the book, *Drunk Tank Pink*, by Adam Alter.

PINK PROFILE

In 1979, Professor Alexander Schauss performed an experiment with 153 men. It was a strength test with an unusual twist. Participants were asked to stare at a piece of blue cardboard and then demonstrate their strength to the researcher. They also stared at a piece of pink cardboard before demonstrating their strength. The results showed that they were "dramatically weaker after staring at the pink cardboard. . . The color pink appeared to leave the men temporarily depleted."

This is hard to believe, and many people didn't believe it. However, other scientists tested Schauss' findings and discovered a similar connection between pink and a reduction in physical strength. This "tranquilizing effect" earned pink a reputation as a "non-drug anesthetic." The reputation is so strong that police departments and correctional facilities started painting holding cells pink. The first to do so, the US Navy, reported "not a single incident during the seven-month trial period." This is the source of the name "drunk tank pink."

More than 300 jails and hospitals use pink rooms, but no one used drunk tank pink more than Joe Arpaio, the controversial sheriff of Maricopa County in Arizona. Known as America's Toughest Sheriff, Arpaio dressed inmates in pink socks and underwear. He also made them dry off with pink towels and sleep on pink sheets.

As Barbara Nemitz explains in *Pink: The Exposed Color in Contemporary Culture,* "pink is one of those colors that clearly influences our behavior." Because of this, many other people and organizations have used pink in an attempt to affect people's actions. In the 1980s, pink paint was used liberally in public housing and was correlated with lower levels of violence. Additionally, volunteers wearing pink received higher donations than those wearing other colors.

College football teams, like the University of Iowa, painted the visiting team's locker rooms pink in order to weaken their rivals before the game (this tactic has now been officially outlawed). Boxers even wore pink trunks in the hope that looking at pink during the fight would reduce the strength of their opponent.

So it seems like pink makes people weak, but maybe it also makes people strong.

In 2017, Krista Suh and Jayna Zweima, the Los Angeles-based founders of the Pussyhat Project, gained notoriety during the Women's March on Washington. Their bright pink and provocatively-shaped hats caught the attention of marchers, the media, and onlookers around the world.

When asked why they chose pink, they said it was "because it was a very female color representing caring, compassion, and love - all qualities that have been derided as weak but are actually STRONG." Similarly, the Susan G. Komen Breast Cancer Foundation declares that "pink is strong, pink is fierce, pink is brave, and pink is mighty."

We'll talk more about the power of pink in a later chapter. Now, let's talk about weirdness...

CHAPTER 2

WHY WEIRDNESS?

Conformity is the ruin of the mind.

— Jesse Shelley

P!NK GOLDF!SH 2.0 is about being weird, strange, unusual, peculiar, different, extraordinary, abnormal, exceptional, uncommon, deviant, unique, unconventional, and odd. It's about standing out and being different.

A lot of people pay lip service to the value of being different and standing out. Many believe it's an essential part of any marketing strategy. However, it is difficult to be different. When you try to be different, there will be pressure to fit in.

If being different is so great, then why isn't every person and every company passionately pursuing it? Robert Quinn argues in *Deep Change* that "deviance will always generate external pressures to conform." Some people see deviance as wrong and dangerous, so they respond with disdain and mockery. It can be risky to stick out. Because of this, we tend to give up on being truly different. Instead, we just do what the competition is doing.

This rejection of deviance doesn't just happen in businesses. In society, pressures to conform are sometimes referred to as leveling mechanisms. They are designed to create social equality and to limit differentiation. Australians and New Zealanders have the "Tall Poppy Syndrome." It is the practice of mocking people who think highly of themselves. If you rise above others, you will get cut down.

In Denmark, they have an entire unofficial code of conduct called the "Law of Jante." The term is borrowed from *A Fugitive Crosses His Tracks*. The book's author, Axel Sandemose, shares the tenets of the law:[3]

- You're not to think you are anything special.
- You're not to convince yourself that you are better than we are.
- You're not to think you are more important than we are.

Being weird can be dangerous and problematic. So why should companies risk being unusual?

Because, it can be even more dangerous to simply remain average. Management guru Tom Peters argues that it is no longer safe to be the same, to be normal, and to be indistinct. Let that sink in for a minute. He is saying that the only safe move—only prudent choice, the only wise decision—is to become unusual, different, strange, and remarkable.

This book is based on the belief that abnormal brands win. But why is it wonderful to be weird? Here are seven reasons to be strange:

BEING NORMAL MAKES YOU ORDINARY
BEING WEIRD MAKES YOU RARE

---

3. https://qz.com/794740/the-happiness-of-the-danes-can-easily-be-explained-by-10-cultural-rules/

Scarcity increases value. Diamonds are valuable primarily because they are rare. Sand and salt are far less valuable, not because they aren't useful, but because they are so ordinary and plentiful. By the way, sand is becoming much more valuable because of its use in semiconductors and concrete. Explosive growth in computing and construction worldwide continues to drive up the price of sand as it becomes more and more scarce.

BEING NORMAL MAKES YOU EASY TO IMITATE
BEING WEIRD MAKES YOU ORIGINAL

Keith Ferrazzi, in his book *Never Eat Alone*, argues that we must "be distinct or be extinct.... The best brands, like the most interesting people, have a distinct message.... When it comes to making an impression, differentiation is the name of the game. Confound expectation. Shake it up."

The value of any product or service immediately decreases once there are acceptable alternatives. An obvious example comes from the world of work. When someone's job can be done faster or cheaper by a computer or an outsourced contractor in another location, that job becomes less valuable. The salary for that position decreases and the likelihood of being replaced increases.

Original brands avoid imitation. They make it difficult to be replaced. There are no good substitutes.

BEING NORMAL MAKES YOU INVISIBLE
BEING WEIRD MAKES YOU NOTICEABLE

Fitting in and following the herd makes us invisible. If we do things well, no one can see us. If our business fits in, everyone drives right by. No one stops. They don't know we're even there. If they do stop, they don't stay long, and they don't buy anything because our products or services are just like everyone else's. If we fit in, we don't get any attention. And attention is one of the most valuable gifts we can get from customers.

Researchers Susan Fiske and Shelley Taylor discovered in 1978 that attention is usually captured by salient, novel, surprising, or distinctive stimuli. This phenomenon is typically called the "Von Restorff Effect." Also called the Isolation Effect, it predicts that when multiple similar objects are present, the one that differs from the rest is the one most likely to be recalled.

BEING NORMAL MAKES YOU PREDICTABLE
BEING WEIRD MAKES YOU SURPRISING

As Chip and Dan Heath explain in *Made to Stick*, we are more likely to be persuaded by messages that are unexpected. If we can surprise someone, we create an emotional reaction and our brains are programmed to respond by releasing dopamine. Dopamine is literally the Post-it Note for our memory. Surprising and delighting a customer generates experiences that are remembered and shared with others.

BEING NORMAL MAKES YOU FORGETTABLE
BEING WEIRD MAKES YOU MEMORABLE

We remember the unusual events in our lives, not the common ones. If no one remembers your brand message, then you don't have the opportunity to influence them. The worst criticism that Simon Cowell, the caustic judge of *American Idol*, can give is that a contestant is forgettable. In contrast, one of his most powerful compliments is that a contestant is memorable. He recently told one female singer, "You are such a strange person. I mean that as a compliment."

The first recorded evidence of odd in English is found in the early 14th century as the adjective odde, meaning "without a corresponding mate." By the late 14th century we see evidence of the word meaning "unconforming, irregular."

The word as applied to people was at first solidly complimentary. If you were odd in a 15th or 16th century kind of way, you were "outstanding, illustrious." It wasn't until the 17th century that the modern sense of odd meaning "peculiar, eccentric" became widely used.

We remember people and businesses that are strange.

BEING NORMAL GIVES PEOPLE NOTHING TO TALK ABOUT
BEING WEIRD MAKES YOU REMARKABLE

When we see something different, we want to tell other people about it. Once people remember your business, the biggest challenge is getting them to tell others about you. As Mark Sanborn demonstrated in *The Fred Factor*, a story about his extraordinary mailman, if you are remarkable enough, someone might even write a book about you. Word of mouth is powerful for both individuals and businesses. If other people are sharing your message, it increases your influence because it enables your message to reach a larger audience.

BEING NORMAL MAKES YOU POWERLESS
BEING WEIRD MAKES YOU INFLUENTIAL

For all the reasons we've just explained, normal organizations have very little power. They are at the mercy of forces beyond their control. However, differentiated businesses are incredibly powerful. Their unique position in the market gives them greater control over their destiny and greater influence with customers and society.

These seven reasons to be strange are clearly demonstrated by an unconventional grocery story with a ridiculous name. Over 100 years ago in Memphis, Tennessee, Clarence Saunders challenged the industry by doing less than all the other grocery stores. We call this Withholding. Before 1916, groceries were sold at stores where a clerk would fetch goods for customers. They'd measure out flour, sugar, and ground coffee beans. They would add up the prices and write them in pencil on the back of the sacks. Even the big chain stores used clerks. Although the chain store model kept costs down, clerks were expensive.

Saunders developed a self-serve model that cut these costs. People selected and transported their own items. Shoppers on that first day did see some employees stocking shelves, but according to the *Tennessee Historical Quarterly*,[4] "They politely refused to select merchandise for visitors." As normal as this seems now, it was unheard of at the time.

By the end of that first year, there were nine locations around Memphis. Saunders called his unique stores Piggly Wiggly. Today, the chain has over 500 grocery stores in 17 states.

Why the weird name? According to the Piggly Wiggly website, "Someone once asked him [Saunders] why he had chosen such an unusual name for his organization, to which he replied, 'So people will ask that very question." Being weird makes Piggly Wiggly remarkable.

PINK PROFILE

"If you want to go unnoticed in a crowd, don't wear pink."

— Mary Quant, fashion designer

Weird is wonderful and pink is weird.

In *Pink: The Exposed Color in Contemporary Culture*, Barbara Nemitz, contends that "pink represents emancipation from the burdens of reality and traditional norms." She points out that pink seldom occurs in nature and is uncommon in architecture and design. Pink "attracts attention by virtue of its rarity in natural environments." Additionally, pink is one of the most infrequently used color terms.

Valerie Steele, in her book, *Pink: The History of a Punk, Pretty, Powerful Color*, argues that "pink always stands out from other colors, making it a special color." She believes that "pink increases visibility in an 'attention economy' where information is increasingly abundant and immediately available. Pink catches the interest of potential consumers." And isn't that the point of marketing, to get the attention and interest of customers?

Now let's explore the metaphors behind the Pink Goldfish starting with the goldfish itself...

---

4. https://www.smithsonianmag.com/smart-news/bizarre-story-piggly-wiggly-first-self-service-grocery-store-180964708/

CHAPTER 3

WHY A GOLDFISH?

"You need to understand the market,
know how you can differentiate yourself in it,
and grasp the functional differentiation competitive points
that are going to allow you to be disruptive."

— Audrey MacLean, founder of Adaptive Corp.

The origin of the goldfish dates back to 2009. It has become a signature part of this book series. Pink is the sixth color in the Goldfish Series. The goldfish represents something small, but despite its size, something with the ability to make a big difference.

The first part of the inspiration for the goldfish came from Kimpton Hotels. The boutique hotel chain introduced something new in 2001. The Hotel Monaco began to offer travelers the opportunity to adopt a temporary travel companion for their stay. Perhaps you were traveling on business and getting a little lonely. Or maybe you were with your family and missing your family pet. Kimpton to the rescue; they gave you a goldfish for your stay. They called the program Guppy Love.

"The 'Guppy Love' program is a fun extension of our pet-friendly nature as well as our emphasis on indulging the senses to heighten the travel experience," said Steve Pinetti, Senior Vice President of Sales & Marketing for Kimpton Hotels and Restaurants, of which Hotel Monaco is part of their premier collection. "Everything about Hotel Monaco appeals directly to the senses, and 'Guppy Love' offers one more unique way to relax, indulge and promote health of mind, body and spirit in our home-away-from-home atmosphere."

> In a publicity stunt, from 1884 to 1894, if you were a resident of Baltimore or Washington, D.C, and wrote your congressman, the US Commission of Fish and Fisheries [today the National Marine Fisheries Service] would send you goldfish. Some 20,000 were given away each year before the program was discontinued.[5]

The second part of our goldfish inspiration came from Stan's first pet. At age six, Stan won "Oscar" at a local fair. Oscar was small and it turns out that the average goldfish is just over three inches in length (10cm). Yet the largest in the world, hailing from The Netherlands, is nearly 19 inches (50cm). That's five times the average size! For comparison, imagine walking down the street and bumping into someone who is three stories tall.

How can there be such a disparity between regular goldfish and their monster cousins? Well, it turns out that the growth of the goldfish is determined by five factors. Just like goldfish, not all businesses grow equally, and we believe that the growth of a product or service faces the same five factors that affect the growth of a goldfish.

5. https://www.nationalgeographic.com/animals/article/history-of-goldfish

1. SIZE OF THE ENVIRONMENT = THE MARKET

GROWTH FACTOR: The size of the bowl or pond.

IMPACT: Direct correlation. The larger the bowl or pond, the larger the goldfish can grow. Similarly, the smaller the market in business, the lesser the growth potential.

2. NUMBER OF OTHER GOLDFISH IN THE BOWL OR POND = COMPETITION

GROWTH FACTOR: The number of goldfish in the same bowl or pond.

IMPACT: Inverse correlation. The more goldfish, the less growth. Similarly, the less competition in business, the more opportunity for growth exists.

3. THE QUALITY OF THE WATER = THE ECONOMY

GROWTH FACTOR: The clarity and amount of nutrients in the water.

IMPACT: Direct correlation. The better the quality, the larger the growth. Similarly, the weaker the economy or capital markets in business, the more difficult it is to grow.

> FACT: A malnourished goldfish in a crowded, cloudy environment may only grow to two inches (six centimeters).

4. THE FIRST 120 DAYS OF LIFE = STARTUP PHASE OR A NEW PRODUCT LAUNCH

GROWTH FACTOR: The nourishment and treatment received as a fry. A fry, as in "small fry" is the term for a baby goldfish.

IMPACT: Direct correlation. The lower the quality of the food, water, and treatment, the more the goldfish will be stunted for future growth. Similarly, in business, the stronger the leadership and capital for a start-up, the better the growth.

5. GENETIC MAKEUP = DIFFERENTIATION

GROWTH FACTOR: The genetic makeup of the goldfish.

IMPACT: Direct correlation. The poorer the genes or the less differentiated, the less the goldfish can grow. Similarly, in business, the more differentiated the product or service from the competition, the better the chance for growth.

FACT: The current *Guinness Book of World Records* holder for the largest goldfish hails from The Netherlands at a whopping 19 inches (50 centimeters). To put that in perspective, that's about the size of the average domestic cat.

WHICH OF THE FIVE FACTORS CAN YOU CONTROL?

Let's assume you have an existing product or service and have been in business for more than four months. Do you have any control over the market, your competition, or the economy? NO, NO, and NO.

The only thing you have control over is your business's genetic makeup or how you differentiate your product or service. In goldfish terms, how do you stand out in a sea of sameness?

PINK PROFILE

We know that goldfish are real, but they aren't pink. They are mostly orange and white. Their color is how they got their name. They look golden in the water. However, it is now possible to have a real pink goldfish.

Pink goldfish are also known as albino goldfish and they are the result of almost 11 years of selective breeding. They are not common, but they do exist. They are rare, which is another reason we chose them for this book.

You can also eat a pink goldfish. Relax. It doesn't involve fishing or cooking, just shopping. Pepperidge Farm sells a Princess Cheddar cracker that comes in a pink package and is filled with tasty little pink goldfish.

Now, why did we choose the color pink?

CHAPTER 4

WHY PINK?

"Pink isn't just a color. It's an attitude too."

— Miley Cyrus

"People usually associate the color pink with weakness and naiveté;
but I associate this color with the most beautiful parts of the day— dawn and dusk.
So pink is strong and wonderful."

— C. JoyBell C.

Pink is the sixth color in the Goldfish series. So why did we choose pink? We've already talked about the connection between pink and weakness, and the relationship between pink and weirdness, but there is so much more.

Let's start with the qualities of pink. What does it mean? What does the color represent? To answer these questions, we did a lot of research. In fact, we read two books completely devoted to the color pink.

Pink: The Exposed Color in Contemporary Art & Culture by Barbara Nemitz focused mostly on the use of pink in paintings and sculptures. *Pink: The History of a Punk, Pretty, Powerful Color* by Valerie Steele was dedicated primarily to clothing and fashion. However, both books also discussed pink in the world as a whole.

Interestingly, we couldn't find much consensus. According to Steele, "pink carries many layers of meaning." That's an understatement. Pink seems to be whatever you think it is or want it to be. Pink was described as both:

- natural and artificial
- pleasurable and unpleasant
- innocent and erotic
- elegant and vulgar
- aristocratic and edgy
- appealing and obscene
- pretty and punk
- vulnerable and powerful
- feminine and masculine
- enjoyable and embarrassing
- novel and eccentric

These inconsistencies are ideal for our purposes. *P!NK GOLDF!SH 2.0* is about how weaknesses can also be strengths, and how apparent flaws can be awesome. Pink is a single color that seems to have many dual and opposing meanings. Perfect.

At the same time, there was some agreement about the essence of pink. Nemitz believes that "pink makes things look more beautiful." Steele seems to concur. They both described pink as sensitive, tender, youthful, emotional, sweet, generous, delicate, sublime, romantic, and happy. Nemitz explains that "we associate pink with flowers, with the sweet, light, transient, and rare."

This might be true in America in the 21st century, but it isn't true everywhere, it hasn't always been true, and it might not be true for much longer. Let's take a look at the surprisingly short history and unusual geography of pink.

Pink didn't used to exist. Well, it existed in nature, but no one had a way of talking about it, at least in the English-speaking world. Pink was first used as a color name in English in the late 1600s. Prior to that, there was no formal recognition that pink was even a color. Some still argue that, scientifically speaking, pink isn't a color because it doesn't exist in the light spectrum.

The golden age for pink was during the Rococo Period in the 1700s. Pastel colors became fashionable in all the courts of Europe. Pink was particularly championed by the mistress of Louis XV, Madame de Pompadour.

Throughout the 1800s and into the early 1900s, pink ribbons or decorations were often worn by young boys in England. That's right. Boys. They were considered small men, and while men in England wore red uniforms, boys wore pink. Pink was seen as a more masculine color than light blue. Let that sink in for a minute. Pink was considered masculine.

A 1918 article explained that "the generally accepted rule is pink for the boys and blue for the girls. The reason is that pink, being a more decided and stronger color, is more suitable for the boy, while blue, which is more delicate and dainty, is prettier for the girl." Pink was strong. Blue was delicate. Theories to explain this have varied over the years, but it's generally believed that blue was associated with the Virgin Mary, hence its more feminine connotations, while pink was linked to red, which was seen as a strong and masculine color.[6]

It wasn't until the mid-1900s that people started choosing pink for girls and blue for boys. This became the accepted norm in the 1940s. The tipping point for pink occurred in 1953. First when the new First Lady of the United States, Mamie Eisenhower, wore a pink gown for the presidential inauguration of her husband, Dwight D. Eisenhower. Then Marilyn Monroe immortalized the color with her iconic pink satin dress while singing *Diamonds Are a Girl's Best Friend*" in the movie *"Gentlemen Prefer Blondes."*

In other words, the current mainstream belief that pink is a female color and that blue is a male color is less than 100 years old. This is important. It hasn't always been this way, and it probably won't be this way for much longer, but we will get to that later. Pink was just getting started.

Steele explains that "the pinkification of girl culture really took off in the 1970s and 1980's when Mattel's Barbie acquired a new, predominantly pink wardrobe." More and more, pink was "associated with youthful femininity." Pop culture continued to drive this association between pink

---

6.   https://www.thevintagenews.com/2019/05/01/pink-blue/

and girls, and as America's cultural influence spread after the Second World War, the American understanding of pink became more universal.

As Nemitz explains, there is a gender divide when it comes to pink. This can be clearly seen in clothing and fashion. "Women tend to find pink quite interesting, while very few men wish to have anything to do with the color. Most men reject pink categorically." Steele agrees. "A pink shirt might be acceptable, but for the most part, pink continues to be unacceptable in the clothing of men."

As recently as 2011, researchers found that girls moved towards pink and boys moved away from pink at a very young age. In a study published by the *British Journal of Developmental Psychology*, it was clear that "by the age of 2.5, girls had a significant preference for the color pink over other colors. At the same time, boys showed an increasing avoidance of pink."

Despite these and other similar findings, sometimes people want to argue that there isn't really a consensus about pink being feminine and blue being masculine. We just have one response to that . . . gender-reveal parties.

At gender-reveal parties throughout the United States (and these parties are becoming more common, not less) attendees and prospective parents wait expectantly for the cake or the balloon or the exploding chalk to reveal the gender of their child. How is this done? Simple. Pink means girl. Blue means boy. When that changes, let us know.

However, the skeptics do have a point. What they really mean is that the associations with pink, and blue, are slowly changing. The lines aren't as clear and as widespread as they used to be. We agree. Just like pink used to be masculine and then it became feminine, it has the ability to keep changing, and it is changing.

Nemitz believes that, in 21st century America, pink "enables those who wear it to set themselves apart from the conventional male image," and that pink clothing gives men "a softer, more approachable look." Kwame Jackson, who finished in second place during the first season of *The Apprentice*, argues that wearing pink "shows confidence in your masculinity." Valerie Steele boldly declares that pink has "accomplished it's gender-bending mission. . . Once pink has been interpreted as an 'androgynous' and 'political' color that speaks to young men and women of all races, these meanings cannot be erased."

Steele goes on to point out that the connection between women and pink was originally strengthened by Hollywood and the film industry. For decades, "pink has been utilized by costume designers to express femininity and hyper-femininity." However, this is also changing.

Michael Kaplan has been a costume designer since 1978. He is best known for his work on *Blade Runner*, *Fight Club*, and *Star Wars: The Last Jedi*. He believes that "pink has strong connotations and makes a statement if used to make a point about the dual nature of femininity." As Steele concludes, "the color pink went from being a feminine pastel to being a bold unisex symbol of rebellion."

This can be seen in some sports. Pink has "reached a critical mass in unexpected places." When many younger players at the 2017 US Open Golf Men's Tournament wore pink pants and pink shirts, it was so surprising that it prompted a *New York Times* fashion article. Vanessa Friedman wrote that "the amount of pink on view on Saturday was impossible to ignore.... This was pink-by-choice, pink as a core element of a competitive wardrobe." She argued that pink has become "a state of mind, or an idea, as opposed to a specific Pantone shade." It is now a "symbol of this particular moment in time, from the looser definitions of gender and gender stereotypes, to the refusal to be boxed in, to a traditional set of dress code mores and expectations."

This is important. Colors don't have a gender. There is nothing inherently feminine or masculine in any particular shade. However, society has ascribed gender to certain colors, and when people challenge these arbitrary categories, it is different. It is unusual. It stands out.

Michel Pastoreau is a professor of medieval history in France. He helps explain the varying beliefs about pink and why they change over time and in other places. "Color is a natural phenomenon . . . . It is society that makes color, defines it, gives it its meaning." In other words, color doesn't mean anything, except what we decide it means in our time and our culture. So far, our discussion has focused on American ideas about pink, but, in other countries, pink is seen very differently.

Valerie Steele found that "pink is a color with a long history in Japan." As we said previously, there wasn't an English word for pink until the 1600s. In contrast, "the Japanese language had a word for the color pink (momo) one thousand years earlier."

In Japan, pink is linked closely with the blooming of the cherry blossom, known as sakura. It is the third favorite color in the entire country. According to Steele, "pink is everywhere in Japan," and it is a "national obsession." Additionally, instead of being seen as a feminine color, Barbara Nemitz found that "Japanese people tend to associate this rather delicate color with masculine themes." Pink is also the color of happiness in Japan.

Similarly, Steele discovered that "India has a special relationship with pink." It is often said that pink is the navy blue of India. Pink doesn't have specific connotations related to gender. "Pink has long been a very popular color in India for both men's and women's clothing and adornment."

One example of India's affinity for and admiration of pink, is Jaipur, also known as the Pink City. With a population of more than three million people, it is the tenth largest city in India. In 2019, UNESCO named Jaipur a World Heritage Site.

This city is unique, historical, and pink because of a visit from the Prince of Wales in 1876. In preparation for the royal visit, the city was painted pink in his honor. Why did they choose pink? At the time, pink was the color of welcome and hospitality.

The pink color scheme has been largely maintained to this day. In fact, it is illegal to paint buildings any other color. A law was passed in 1877 that enforces the continuous use of pink. We admire that commitment. Stan actually visited Jaipur in 2003 and Dave hopes to visit soon.

Cultural and historical ideas about pink affect the way it is perceived and used in organizations. Pink has been used very effectively as a differentiator by an interesting mix of nonprofits and businesses.

BREAST CANCER AWARENESS

In 1985, October was designated by the American Cancer Society as National Breast Cancer Awareness Month. The Susan G. Komen Foundation distributed pink ribbons to breast cancer survivors in 1991 at the annual Race for the Cure. The Breast Cancer Research Foundation chose a pink ribbon as their symbol in 1993. Since then, the month of October and the color pink have become synonymous with the cause of breast cancer research and treatment. Each October, male and female athletes wear pink to raise awareness for the cause.

Let's focus on this example for a moment because it illustrates clearly our reasons for using pink. It's remarkable when National Football League players wear pink. When big, tough guys wear pink, people notice. This is because, as we have discussed, most people think of pink as a feminine color and therefore, it's unusual to see men wearing pink, especially when they are wearing helmets and trying to physically destroy each other.

@GIANTFREAKINPINK

David Rendall is the ultimate advocate for embracing weirdness and exploiting imperfection. David wears head to toe pink on stage. This includes pink pants, pink shoes, pink socks, pink belt, and a pink watch. His shirts display his trademark pink Tyrannosaurus Rex. He even has a custom-made three-piece pink pinstripe suit, which he wears with a pink shirt, pink tie, and pink Chuck Taylor shoes. He is @giantfreakinpink on *Instagram.*

When asked about all the pink, David credits his family with the inspiration. He and his wife, Stephanie, have three beautiful daughters, Sophia, Emma, and Anna. Even his dog Snowbell is a female. During his speeches, he tells a series of funny stories about how living in a house full of women is gradually turning him into a woman. From pushing him to use an exfoliating body wash to painting his toenails to telling him to trim his eyebrows, David believes they were on a mission

Photo Credit: Simpleview Summit

to make him more like them. Instead of pushing back, he has chosen to embrace his feminine side and the color that represents it—pink.

His unconventional commitment to pink makes him memorable to his audiences. David leaned in and pink has become inextricably linked to his brand. It's on the cover of his book. It's on his website. It's everywhere, even off-stage. Because he competes in Ironman triathlons and ultramarathons, he had his bike custom-painted pink. He also has a pink helmet, sunglasses, hat, tri-suit, and socks. Even his wedding ring is pink, thanks to Qalo.

Pink is the main differentiator for him. It makes him remarkable. David powers his business on referrals. He gets audience members to say, "You've got to hear this guy. He's funny and he wears pink pants and he talks about dyslexic billionaires and freakish arm wrestlers from Germany." More than once David has been approached in an airport by someone who recognized him because of his pink clothes. David receives pink gifts from his clients and fans, most notably, pink underwear and a pink cowboy hat. His *Instagram* feed is a constant barrage of interesting pink objects, like cars and buildings, sent from people all over the world.

But it didn't start this way. David didn't always wear pink. He didn't always want to stick out. He didn't want to be weird. He wanted to be normal and professional. He wanted to be accepted. He wanted to fit in. He wore normal pants, normal shirts, normal shoes, and normal ties. He wanted to meet other people's conceptions of what a successful person wore. He wanted people to take him seriously.

It's hard sometimes to go against the grain of what everybody else does because we wonder if people are going to like it. That is why we wrote this book. We want to show you the power of pink, the power of being different, the power of defying expectation, and the power of being weird.

It wouldn't be fair or consistent to tell other people to be freaks and to pursue an extraordinary path to success while behaving and dressing in a completely conventional way. This is another reason David started wearing pink. He had to practice what he preached. He had to walk the talk. He had to eat his own Pink Goldfish food. He wanted to experiment, in his life and business, with the value of being strange. His experience has convinced him that there is tremendous value in living an uncommon life.

Dave gets some feedback that he's gone too far with pink. People suggest that he should dial it back. A little pink is fun and different, but they think too much could be a problem. This is interesting, because maybe he hasn't gone far enough. Maybe he'd have even more success if he were even more pink. We'll discuss this more in the Lopsiding chapter.

David isn't the only one who's found an advantage in being pink. Let's look at a handful of other companies who've leveraged the color.

PINK-TRASH

Kelly Buffalino started Pink-Trash in Wilmington, North Carolina, because she was unhappy with the poor service and high fees of other providers. She created a company focused on better service, environmental values, and low flat rates.

She chose pink because it's "her favorite color and the high visibility attracts new customers." As a breast cancer survivor, Kelly is also committed to supporting cancer treatment for local men and women. Her company does this through donations of time, money, and resources.

PINK SNOW PLOWS

While working on finalizing the first edition of *Pink Goldfish*, David was a speaker at the Michigan Green Industry Association's annual trade show. As he walked to the ballroom, he felt a little conspicuous in his pink pants and pink shoes. All of the attendees were in the landscaping and snow removal business. As far as their dress, it was a sea of blue, green, black, and gray. There weren't a lot of bright colors, especially in the middle of winter. He wasn't sure this was an audience that would appreciate his pink wardrobe.

As he was standing in the back of the room, waiting to go on stage, he bumped into the founder of Troy Clogg Landscape Associates. Troy said he loved the pink and explained that his employees wear pink uniforms and drive pink snow plows and pink trucks. They also sell pink road salt. Hot

Pink Deicer is another company they founded and profits from each sale allow them to donate thousands of dollars each year to breast cancer patients who are struggling financially.

Talk about standing out. Have you ever seen a pink snow plow? Troy has learned that it pays to do things differently than everyone else in his industry, and pink is a key part of his differentiation strategy. It's also part of his mission to help cancer patients and their families.

OWENS CORNING

Owens Corning has been leveraging pink for nearly 65 years. The insulation and building-products company uses the color in its insulation products and carries the trademarked value of pink on its balance sheet.

That idea of differentiating its products was the driving force behind adding the pink color to the insulation. Red dye was used in part to distinguish the new insulation from other kinds.

In an article with *The Blade*, former VP Joe Doherty shared, "I don't think we ever realized the power of pink in the marketplace. It was about differentiating with customers. Then we realized we had something different on our hands — it was the color."[7]

PINK PROFILE

Pink is what I do.
Alecia is who I am.
The world has taken Pink
and turned it into this thing,
a brand - a snarl.

— Alecia Beth Moore (aka P!NK)

Raise your glass
if you are wrong
in all the right ways.

— From the song, *Raise Your Glass*

---

7. https://www.toledoblade.com/Retail/2013/10/27/Pink-Panther-color-carry-considerable-value-in-Owens-Corning-marketing-efforts.html

Please don't you ever feel like you're
less than, less than perfect.
If you ever feel like you're nothing,
you are perfect to me.

— From the song, *F**kin' Perfect*

There is no better representative for the color pink than P!NK, the Grammy award winning singer and songwriter, but she wasn't always pink. Her given name is Alecia Beth Moore.

In 1995, her first album was certified double-platinum after it sold more than two million copies. She has continued her music career for more than 25 years. *Hurts 2B Human*, her most recent album, was released in 2019 and she has now sold more than 90 million albums. Her many awards include *Billboard's* Woman of the Year in 2013 and #10 on *VH1's* 100 Greatest Women in Music.

P!NK didn't change her name in a sophisticated attempt to brand herself. "It's just a nickname that's been following me my whole life. It started off as a mean thing." After being publicly humiliated at camp, she blushed so intensely that everyone started teasing her and calling her Pink.

Years later, in the very popular film, *Reservoir Dogs*, Mr. Pink was a character played by Steve Buscemi with a "smart mouth." This fit with her personality and confirmed her status as P!NK.

You might also notice that we borrowed her use of the exclamation point as a replacement for the letter i on the cover of our book.

Now that we've explored the meaning behind pink and goldfish, the next part of the book will focus on uncovering the eight different Pink Goldfish strategies.

Are you ready to be F.L.A.W.S.O.M.E? Let's go...

SECTION II

THE TYPES (THE WHAT)

CHAPTER 5

DISCOVERING F.L.A.W.S.O.M.E

"Most of us spend our lives trying to be, and seem, 'perfect.'
We try to protect ourselves.
It can sometimes be difficult to drop the pretense
and own up to your flaws and faults –
it takes courage."

— Brené Brown, *The Gifts of Imperfection*

In the 15th century the Japanese Shogun Ashikaga Yoshimasa sent for his favorite tea bowl. The broken bowl was in the process of being repaired. When it came back, it was fixed using ugly metal staples and other coarse black glue. His heart sank. This wasn't acceptable.

Ashikaga called in his best craftsmen from all of the Osaka region. He handed over the bowl and challenged them to find a more aesthetically pleasing method of repair. The craftsmen carefully took apart the previously fixed bowl. They removed the staples and the ugly glue. After cleaning each piece, they began to use lacquer and gold to meticulously repair the cracks. The entire process took two weeks.

The craftsmen returned and presented the tea bowl. Ashikaga's heart leapt as he held it in his hands. The shogun was extremely pleased with the result.

KINTSUGI

Born out of the efforts of these craftsmen came the art of Kintsugi. It is the practice of repairing broken pottery with lacquer dusted or mixed with powdered gold, silver, or platinum.

Photo Credit: Shutterstock

Kintsugi in Japanese translates to "golden joinery."[8] It has become a metaphor for embracing your breaks and flaws. It espouses the idea that the broken is more beautiful than the pristine. The gold is used to intentionally call attention to the breaks instead of concealing them.

Collectors became so enamored with the new art that some were accused of deliberately smashing valuable pottery so it could be repaired with the golden seams of Kintsugi.

Here is the important takeaway from the art form of Kintsugi. Mending the cracks makes the object more beautiful, not despite the flaws, but because of attention placed on them. This is the crux of the reasoning behind the Pink Goldfish concept—embracing what makes you weird or weak.

> "Perfection is sort of boring. I take the perfect for granted. I'm way more interested, and spend far more time and money on the imperfect things, the things that might not work, the ideas and services, and products that dance around the edges. If you're going to offer something that's imperfect, by all means, make it as good as you possibly can, but embrace the fact that you're not selling perfect. You're selling interesting."
>
> — Seth Godin

PORTMANTEAU

A portmanteau is a French word for a small suitcase. It also describes when parts of multiple words are combined to make a new word. For example, by blending smoke and fog to create smog. Or vlog, from video, web, and log. A portmanteau relates to a singular concept that the combined word describes. A portmanteau differs from a compound word, which does not involve the truncation of parts of the stems of the blended words.

The portmanteau we use for a Pink Goldfish is FLAWSOME. It is a combination of FLAWS and AWESOME—the simple idea that your flaws hold the key to what makes you awesome. The concept of flawsome isn't new. The term was originated by Trendspotting,[9] the supermodel Tyra Banks, and motivational speaker Erik Qualman in 2012. Let's look at each source:

According to Trendspotting in 2012, consumers don't expect brands to be flawless. In fact, consumers will embrace brands that are FLAWSOME. Brands that are still brilliant despite having flaws; even being flawed (and being open about it) can be awesome.

---

8. https://en.wikipedia.org/wiki/Kintsugi
9. http://trendwatching.com/trends/pdf/2012-03 FLAWSOME.pdf

According to Tyra Banks, FLAWSOME is used to describe something that is awesome because of its flaws. She advocates for us to embrace the flaws in our bodies and own them for they are simply flawsome. Tyra launched the Flawsome Ball to benefit her TZONE Foundation in 2012.[10]

Erik Qualman believes FLAWSOME is about learning from our mistakes. Through our flaws we can actually showcase how awesome we really are – whether it be as individuals or as a company. He advocates for using your failures to humanize your personal or corporate brand.

More Than a Portmanteau

In addition to the flawsome portmanteau, we've chosen to make an acronym out of it. Each letter in the F.L.A.W.S.O.M.E. framework represents one of the eight different types of Pink Goldfish:

F is for Flaunting

L is for Lopsiding

A is for Antagonizing

W is for Withholding

S is for Swerving

O is for Opposing

M is for Micro-weirding

E is for Exposing

F.L.A.W.S.O.M.E. MATRIX

We've also created a matrix to illustrate how to become F.L.A.W.S.O.M.E.

The vertical Y axis in the matrix stands for the amount of perfection or imperfection:

10. https://www.rachaelrayshow.com/celebs/8265_Tyra_Banks_Flawsome_Ball_Celebration_of_the_Muffin_Top/

IMPERFECT

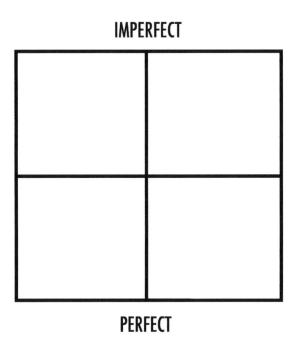

PERFECT

Imperfection is what makes you different or unique in business. Being imperfect is usually seen as a weakness or a flaw because it doesn't conform to the established model of success. Doing something abnormal is often seen as doing it the "wrong way."

Perfect represents the standards within your industry. Perfect defines the "right way." It is usually synonymous with strong. If everyone is doing it, then it must be a good thing.

The X axis represents doing "more" or doing "less" of what makes you either perfect or imperfect:

IMPERFECT

LESS 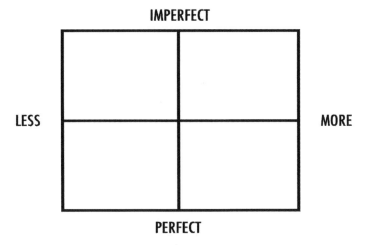 MORE

PERFECT

UNDERSTANDING THE QUADRANTS

The F.L.A.W.S.O.M.E. matrix contains four quadrants:

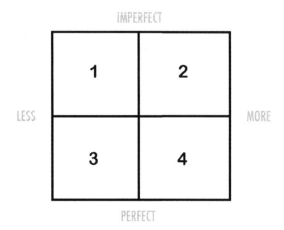

Each quadrant in the matrix is represented by an animal. The first quadrant, the top left, represents doing less of what is considered perfect. It is the **COW** quadrant:

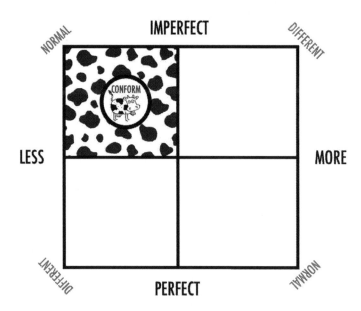

Why a Cow? Every cow is unique. Their spots are like our fingerprints. No two cows are alike. Yet, cows are blissfully unaware of their uniqueness. Establish a cowpath and cows will never stray from it. This is the CONFORM quadrant.

The second quadrant, the top right, represents doing more of what seems imperfect. It is called the **PEACOCK** quadrant:

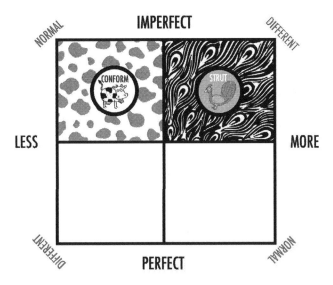

Why a Peacock? Like cows and their spots, the feathers on a peacock are unique. Unlike cows, they own it. Their uniqueness is a signature part of who they are. They purposefully preen and flaunt their feathers to stand out among the flock. This is the STRUT quadrant.

The third quadrant, the bottom right, represents doing more of what is considered perfect. It is the **ZEBRA** quadrant:

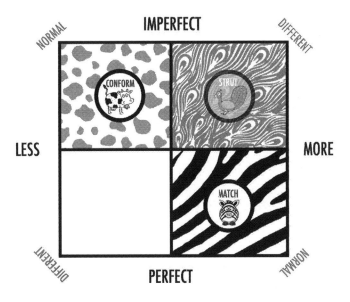

Why a Zebra? Zebras are black with white stripes. Their striping is determined by genetics. Even though zebras are unique, their individual stripes are indistinguishable among other zebras. Their stripes create a blending effect, making it impossible for an individual zebra to stand out among the herd. This is good for safety as predators see the herd as one huge object, but it makes standing out a non-starter. You can't add stripes and be different here. It's just more of the same. This is the MATCH quadrant.

The fourth quadrant, the bottom left, represents doing less of what is considered perfect. It is the **POLAR BEAR** quadrant:

Why a Polar Bear? What color are Polar bears? Contrary to popular belief, they aren't white. They are black. Their fur is translucent because each individual hair is hollow. The fur absorbs the light and takes away all of the colors in the spectrum so they appear white. Generally, polar bears avoid the herd and live solitary lives. This is the SUBTRACT quadrant.

If you truly want to stand out, you need to be like a peacock and a polar bear. Own what makes you different and not be afraid to avoid following what is considered "normal" in business.

Are you a 3 percenter?

It turns out that only 3 percent of people and brands have the ability to become extraordinary.

Paul Rulkens in his 2014 TEDx Maastricht talk[11] points out that the majority is almost always wrong. It's because they live within the box. The lines that shape the box are the boundaries and standards we live by. We get hampered by "industry" norms (Legal, Moral, Social, Ethical, etc.)

---

11. https://www.youtube.com/watch?v=VNGFep6rncY

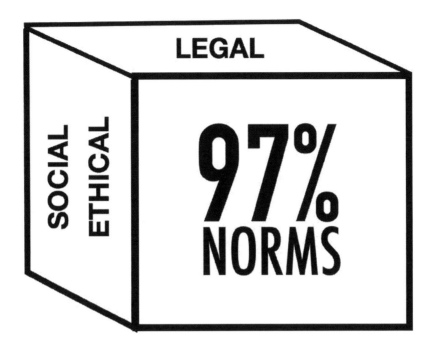

Or we begin to conform and benchmark the leaders by emulating their attributes. Remember the Zebra quadrant? This isn't a path to innovation. It's a recipe for sameness. Most companies practice R&D as if it stands for Ripoff & Duplicate.

What's the answer? How do you stand out? According to Rulkens,

> You need to know the word norm is an abbreviation for normal. In other words, if you do what everyone else is doing you get results that everyone else is getting. And those aren't normal results and the thing is what we are after today are extraordinary results. So, the key question is 'How can you kick yourself out of this very small box of your industry and professional field and move to the happy place where cool innovation happens?'

You can become part of that 3 percent by deciding as of today to break your industry standards and norms. This is the essence of Pink Goldfish strategy. Do MORE of what makes you weird or intentionally do LESS of what everyone considers normal in your industry. Do MORE of what your customers value and unapologetically LESS of what they don't.

Next, let's explore each of the letters in F.L.A.W.S.O.M.E. The F of Flaunting is first...

CHAPTER 6

FLAUNTING

"If you can't fix it, feature it."

— Gerald Weinberg

THE "F" IN F.L.A.W.S.O.M.E. STANDS FOR FLAUNTING

Flaunt means to parade, show off, display, strut, or be ostentatious. It's also about being unashamed or being proud of something. Our interpretation of the word is positive. Flaunting is about being unapologetic about your organization's flaws. You take pride in your organization's unique characteristics. You emphasize them, accentuate them, feature them, highlight them, expose them, call attention to them, and openly display them. You definitely aren't trying to hide them or fix them.

Too often, we are uncomfortable with what makes us weird. Our goal in this book isn't simply to help you become comfortable with what makes you weak or weird in business and in life. We want you to parade those weaknesses without shame, to show them off.

This might sound unwise, because this isn't the way most organizations operate. It isn't what most business books recommend. Managers have been taught to find and fix weakness, to seek perfection.

FINDING STRENGTH IN WEAKNESS

Established in 1919, W.K. Buckley formulated a cough syrup called Buckley's Mixture. Noted for its strongly unpleasant taste, its ingredients include ammonium carbonate, potassium bicarbonate, camphor, menthol, Canada balsam, pine needle oil, and a tincture of capsicum. Translation: the mixture tastes horrible and is not for the faint of heart. Look on *Amazon* for reviews of Buckley's Mixture and you'll find:

Reviewed by Dreadlocgrl

5.0 out of 5 stars

Great for people with nagging coughs

It does what it is intended to do. Great for people with nagging coughs.

Buckley's is superb for asthmatics because it aids in clearing congestion. I have been using this product since the age of 5 years old and it has never failed to disappoint me....

For those who complain it tastes nasty, SUCK IT UP BUTTERCUP!!!!! Just take a Buckley's shot straight no chaser and you will be fine.

Reviewed by AMAZONIAN

5.0 out of 5 stars

Ever Drink Drain Cleaner?

This stuff is renowned for its awful flavor (apparently - I'd never heard of it - the wife bought it for me) and with good reason. Ammonia. It contains a type of it, I think, and tastes like "smelling salts" (ammonia) smells. God-awful.

Not sure how it works on cough yet because after one taste, my body decided it would rather never cough again than to have to taste this again. SO I GUESS IT WORKS!!!

Reviewed by Sarah K Bilby

5.0 out of 5 stars

Tastes Like a Horror, Works Like a Wonder

Take the worst thing you have ever tasted and multiply that times a thousand and you're not anywhere close to how bad this stuff tastes, but it calms and soothes my cough like nothing else. I have tried Delsym and it doesn't even touch my cough. Buckley's may taste like liquefied death, but it leaves a cooling sensation that helps quell your cough. I chase my dose with a tablespoon of honey, and this works quite nicely for me.

After W.K.'s death in 1978, Buckley's adopted son, Frank, became the president of the company. In the mid-1980s, Frank became the spokesperson for the brand. He commissioned research and found that Buckley's was notorious for two reasons. Consumers consistently spoke to its efficacy and its lousy taste. Frank decided to flaunt the taste and began promoting a new slogan for the brand, "It tastes awful. And it works.

Their cough syrup is nasty, and they are proud of that. Buckley's didn't try to hide it or mask the flavor, like the competition. Instead, they made the bad taste their focus. In advertisements, Frank compared the taste in blind taste tests to trash bag leakage and sweaty gym socks. The implicit message is that it works because it tastes awful.

The bad taste campaign increased Buckley's market share by over 550 percent in the Canadian cough & cold category. The campaign won numerous advertising awards and was subsequently launched in the Caribbean, Australia, New Zealand, and the United States.[12]

---

12. http://www.buckleys.ca/about/history

In 2002, the brand was acquired by Novartis. Kironmoy Datta, senior brand manager for Novartis Consumer Health, says that "Buckley's isn't for everyone.... We made a conscious choice to not be everything to everyone."[13] It takes courage to call attention to existing weaknesses, but it takes even more courage to make those weaknesses appear worse, to exaggerate and flaunt them.

Sometimes a Pink Goldfish tastes unapologetically awful.

Back in 2013, Buckley's was not available for sale in the US due to factory issues. At the time, it had been reputed to sell on *eBay* for 10 times the original price.

THE FLAUNTING ZONE

We will advocate for staying within the "flaunting zone" to differentiate yourself in business:

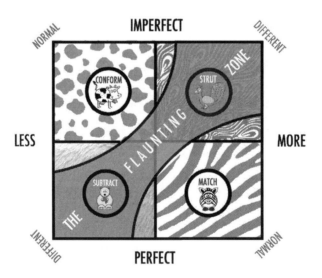

The goal is to flaunt that you do LESS of what is considered perfect *or* flaunt that you do MORE of what seems imperfect.

If you don't believe us that your flaws indeed are the things that make you awesome, then we ask you to consult two of the greatest philosophers and artists of our time:

---

13. http://onwardmag.com/how-flaunting-your-weaknesses-can-build-trust/

Kanye West believes that:

Bob Ross believes that:

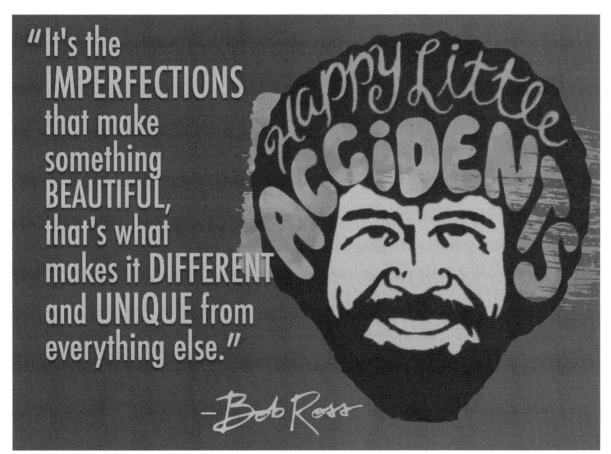

FLAUNTING YOUR WEIRDNESS AND WEAKNESS

Let's look at companies that embrace the concept of Flaunting.

SHITI takes on a YETI - Founded in 2006, YETI is an American outdoor manufacturer company based in Austin, Texas. The premium brand specializes in products such as ice chests, vacuum-insulated stainless-steel drink ware, soft coolers, and related accessories. YETI has lopsided the engineering of their products, and that engineering and branding doesn't come cheap. Some may even accuse YETI of being ridiculously overpriced.

Enter SHITI. In 2016, brothers Austin and Trevor Zacny became sensitive to the popularity of overpriced cooler brands. Nostalgic about their old reliable cooler, they began to realize that the meaning of a cooler was worth much more than how long it held ice. As a joke, Trevor placed a napkin over his older Coleman cooler.

Photo Credit: *YouTube*

He shared a *Snapchat* video with the narration, "Who needs a YETI, when you got a SHITI." Soon after, the youngest Zacny brother, Luke, designed the logo. Stickers were ordered and a business based on Flaunting was launched.

In their words, "We founded SHITI Coolers with a basic mission: To keep using that same damn cooler with the rusted lid and squeaky hinges in hope there were more people out there just like us. A simple SHITI sticker was enough to represent the lifestyle in which we've been living for years. We don't care if your cooler can withstand a grizzly bear or hold ice for 3 weeks. We care about coolers that have been passed down through generations with a story behind them."

The company has grown over the last five years beyond stickers. *WildlyWeakCoolers.com* now offers apparel, nameplates, coolers, cups, and accessories. "As below-average outdoorsmen ourselves, all we wanted was to pack a cooler full of piss warm beer and cast the pole after a long workday. We realized the old rusted cooler we took on countless family trips was doing the job just fine."

Sometimes a Pink Goldfish is a clever spoof on an overpriced cooler.

RyanAir embraces unpopularity – RyanAir flew for the first time in Ireland in 1984. Since then they have grown into Europe's biggest carrier. The company has always prided itself on cheap no-frills flights. However, it fundamentally fails to deliver a positive flying experience for consumers, and its customer service is famed for its bad attitude.

RyanAir routinely tops the consumer surveys for the least popular airline, an honor it received again in 2019 for the seventh straight year. CEO Michael O'Leary is renowned for his controversial comments, such as, "We don't want to hear your sob stories." or "What part of 'no refund' don't you understand?" According to *Forbes*, likeability isn't integral to his leadership style.[14]

Does RyanAir make excuses for the poor level of service? Absolutely not. They flaunt it. In 2013, the brand launched its very own "*I Hate Ryanair*" website.

Here are just a few of the things customers complain about:

- a 70 euro charge to print a boarding pass at the airport
- reducing the number of airplane bathrooms
- no seat back pockets

---

14. https://www.forbes.com/sites/forbescoachescouncil/2017/07/19/why-we-only-need-one-degree-shifts-in-life-and-business/2/

- no water served on flights
- a six euro charge to pay with a credit card
- no air sickness bags
- a clunky website
- inconvenient airport locations

Instead of trying to resolve these complaints, RyanAir uses their negative reputation to threaten further reductions in service. These empty threats generate additional free publicity. Here are a few examples of changes they announced, but had no intention of actually implementing:

- charging one euro to use the toilet
- creating a standing-room-only section
- requiring passengers to carry checked luggage to the plane
- charging overweight passengers a fat tax

Even though they pledged to change their ways in 2014, they still ended 2017 as the lowest-rated airline in Europe. This was due to their handling of massive flight cancellations during the holiday season. They've also been ranked as the worst service of any company in Europe, not just the worst airline. In January 2018, they announced new size restrictions and charges for carry-on bags. Only one (very) small bag is allowed for free. Any additional bags will cost at least five euros.

O'Leary was asked if he was concerned about their negative corporate image. He responded with this provocative statement. "Our booking engine is full of passengers who have sworn they will never fly with us again." Flying RyanAir will save you money, but it will be painful. They know it and they flaunt it.

Sometimes a Pink Goldfish is an airline everyone loves to hate.

Mini embraces small – Americans love big vehicles. Big trucks and SUVs are the preferred means of transportation for millions of US drivers. That fact made BMW's introduction of the Mini to the United States very interesting.

What would they do? Would they downplay the car's small size? At the time, it was about two feet shorter than the average compact car. Would they ignore size and focus on other features? Nope.

They flaunted its tiny proportions. They exaggerated how little it was by comparing it to mobile phones and by putting a Mini in the bed of a pickup truck.

As YoungMe Moon explains in *Different - Escaping the Competitive Herd*, "It took its biggest possible wart and made it even bigger. All of its advertising seems to say 'it's even smaller than you think.'" This was intentional.

Alex Bogusky and his ad agency, Crispin Porter + Bogusky (CP+B), have been the creators of many well-known advertising campaigns. Among those was the introduction of the Mini to America. Its success was based on flaunting the weaknesses of Mini, not minimizing them. Instead of hiding qualities that seemed negative—such as its tiny proportions—CP+B exploited them.

According to Bogusky, "It's part of your job as a marketer to find the truths in a company, and you let them shine through in whatever weird way it might be. Naturally, that risks pissing someone off." Mini is small. It's obvious from the name. So, they flaunted it.

Sometimes a Pink Goldfish is a tiny car that fits in the trunk of your other car.

"We have more HVAC providers per capita than we do teachers! Not sure if that fun fact is actually a fact; the point is we have a lot of HVAC providers, so it's really important to stand out."

Thanks to Zachary Milito for sharing the Pink Goldfish example of Goettle Air Conditioning & Plumbing. Zach is based in the Valley of the Sun. Goettl is an industry pioneer in Phoenix.

The company was founded in 1939, when Gust and Adam Goettl developed the Phoenix area's first evaporative cooler and refrigerated AC unit. Since then the company has been battling the severe desert temperatures.

In Zach's words, "I saw the attached billboard the other day and thought of you, more specifically about your Pink Goldfish presentation at AMA Michiana. I think this would qualify as "Flaunting"... what do you think?"

Continued...

Photo Credit: Zachary Milito

Our answer: ABSOLUTELY.

Flaunting is about being unashamed or being proud of something. You take pride in your unique characteristics. You emphasize them, accentuate them, call attention to them, and openly display them.

Goettl is an unusual name. The company has even made a jingle out of it:

"Geottl. G-O-E-T-T-L. Geottl. It's really hard to spell."

Bud Light and Sam Adams flaunt their differences - It's 5 o'clock somewhere people, how do you stand out in the beer garden?

Let's look at different approaches from Bud and Sam:

Bud Light flaunts that they are for "The Many." The many who are turned off by the few who insist picking a beer is akin to fine wine. In the *"Dilly, Dilly"* campaign, here is the dialogue from one of the spots:

King: "Barkeep, Bud Lights for everyone!"

Guest: "Actually, I prefer a nice mead."

King: "Barkeep, Bud Lights for everyone and one mead."

Guest: "Is it autumnal?"

King: "Barkeep, Bud Lights for everyone and one autumnal mead."

Guest: "Is it malty and full-bodied because I like——"

King: "Cancel that mead."

Tagline: "Bud Light. For the Many, Not the Few" over the Guest shackled in the stocks.

Photo Credit: YouTube

Sam Adams

Bud Light is for the many, not the few. Sam Adams is for the few, not the many. Efficiency is important for the right things, the things that matter the most to your customers and employees, but, maybe deliberate inefficiency can be a strength.

Boston Beer Company flaunts that Sam Adams has been, "Brewed Inefficiently since 1984." According to a blog post by Tim Williams, "This classic Boston beer brand allows extra time for its hops to fully mature in order to craft its full-flavored lager. Sam Adams could have a more 'efficient' brewing process, but it would result in a much less satisfying product."[15]

Sometimes a Pink Goldfish is a beer that's unapologetic or inefficient.

---

15. https://www.ignitiongroup.com/linkedin-articles/your-clients-pay-you-to-be-effective-not-efficient

According to Tim Williams, "An efficiency expert visiting an Apple store might reasonably conclude that Apple could pack in a lot more products into a lot less space — these spacious stores are famously sparse. But this 'inefficient' use of space produces the highest sales per square foot of any retailer in the world."

Personal Branding Profile

Jimmy Vee at Gravitational Marketing calls himself "The Five-Foot High Marketing Guy." He doesn't try to hide his short stature. Jimmy flaunts it and celebrates it. It makes him likable, memorable, and interesting.

Flaunting is genetic for Jimmy. After finishing college, he created a seven-page, non-traditional resume with an advertorial as a cover letter.

According to *GravitationalMarketing.com*, "Everyone told him that his resume was a joke and that he'd never get a job—resumes are only supposed to be one page, according to the know-it-alls at the college! But before he even graduated, that seven-page resume landed him a job as the assistant to the Vice President at a Direct Response Advertising Agency."[16] This is a great example of Lopsiding, which we'll introduce in the next chapter.

Sometimes a Pink Goldfish is a short ad man.

PINK PROFILE

Remember Krista Suh and Jayna Zweima, the Los Angeles-based founders of the Pussyhat Project? They are a great example of flaunting, declaring that "wearing pink together is a powerful statement that we are unapologetically feminine and we unapologetically stand for women's rights."

The perception of pink as a symbol has undergone a major transformation over the last century. A pink triangle-shaped patch was used in Nazi concentration camps to identify

---

16. https://gravitationalmarketing.com/#jimtravis

homosexuals. It was intended as a badge of shame, a way of identifying them as deviants to their fellow prisoners, the color pink denoting their lack of masculinity.

However, since then, pink has been reshaped into a symbol of resistance and a symbol of gay rights. An example of this is ACT UP, the AIDS Coalition to Unleash Power, which uses pink triangles in their logos and on their posters. From shame to pride, from powerless to powerful, pink is unapologetic.

The F in F.L.A.W.S.O.M.E. is Flaunting, parading without shame. Let's move on to the L...

CHAPTER 7

LOPSIDING

*"True differentiation is rarely a function of
well-roundedness;
it is typically a function of lopsidedness."*

— Youngme Moon, *Different: Escaping the Competitive Herd*

THE "L" IN F.L.A.W.S.O.M.E. STANDS FOR LOPSIDING

Most brands are trying to be balanced and well-rounded. It's interesting to note that synonyms for balanced include: sane, right, normal, and stable. Those sound like worthy goals. Be the perfect amount of everything. Be the best of both worlds. Make everyone happy. Eliminate flaws, minimize them, decrease them, diminish them, and lessen them. We think this is the wrong approach.

Lopsiding is about being unbalanced, imperfect, unstable, and odd. Let's stop here for a second. Antonyms for unbalanced include: crazy, insane, and unsound. Those don't sound like promising descriptions of brand strategy, but bear with us. Lopsiding involves amplifying, not reducing, your brand's flaws. We want you to expand them, magnify them, increase them, turn them up, exaggerate them, and then supersize them.

Lopsiding is on one of the two extreme ends of the flaunting zone.

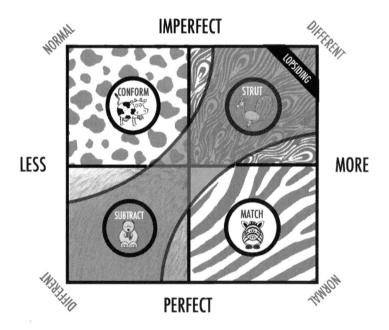

Brands here are purposefully doing MORE of what makes them imperfect. This is flaunting imperfection at its best. You aren't just proud of your weaknesses, you are expanding and extending them. You are doubling down to accentuate your flaws.

Lopsiding is not for the faint of heart. It takes courage to call attention to existing weaknesses. It takes even more courage to make those weaknesses worse, to exaggerate them. That's what Hardee's did, and it saved their company.

Here is a letter from Andy Puzder, former CEO of CKE Restaurants (parent of Carl's Jr. and Hardee's), on the back of a bag for a Philly Cheesesteak Thickburger:

> When I became president of Hardee's Restaurants, we were selling so many things that we had truly become a 'jack of all trades and master of none.' Unfortunately, in today's competitive fast food world, that wasn't cutting it. The chain needed to become known for doing something really well again. So I challenged my menu development folks to come up with a new line of burgers that would make people say 'Wow! I can't believe I can get burgers that good at a fast-food place.' And they did. They came up with Thickburgers.

What is a Thickburger? It is a very large hamburger (up to 2/3 pounds) with generous amounts of other toppings. The All-American Thickburger is topped with a full hot dog and potato chips as well as lettuce, tomato, mayo, ketchup, onions, and pickles. The Philly Cheesesteak Thickburger piles an already unhealthy sandwich on top of an unhealthy hamburger to form a monster that contains enough calories to fuel the average person for about a week. By the way, our description isn't hyperbole. Hardee's also sells a Monster Thickburger. New Thickburger varieties are regularly released and others are retired.

Hardee's didn't stop with the Thickburger. Their newest outrageous creation is our personal favorite, the Aporkalypse. It combines all parts of the pig, ham, sausage, and bacon on a biscuit or a burrito. The name says it all. Eating this franken-food will probably end your life, but it will be worth it.

It is important to note that Carl's Jr. and Hardee's were closing many of their stores before developing this new line of burgers. Even more importantly, most other fast food companies were furiously adding healthy options to their menu as a result of the Morgan Spurlock documentary *Supersize Me*. In response to criticism about the negative health effects of their offerings, fast food outlets were offering water, fruit, yogurt, and salads. Hardee's moved in the opposite direction. In essence, they were saying, "our food is fat and nasty and will make you fat and nasty." And it worked.

They succeeded by amplifying the weaknesses of fast food while everyone else was busy trying to moderate those same weaknesses. They took fast food, which was already tremendously unhealthy, and they lopsided it to make it even unhealthier. They took fatty foods and made them fattier. They took nasty food and made it nastier.

Hardee's also made their advertising nastier. They are infamous for sexually suggestive advertisements that have led to criticism from various groups, but apparently not from their core customers. We call this Antagonizing and it is the subject of the next chapter.

Hardee's also antagonizes vegetarians and vegans in their "Save the Veggies" campaign. Seemingly serious spokespeople standing in endless fields of green ask viewers to save the vegetables by eating their new roast beef sandwich. They demand sympathy for the helpless lettuce and carrots that are needlessly slaughtered each day.

Sometimes a Pink Goldfish is wrapped in bacon and covered in sausage.

McDonald's can't make you healthy – This chapter started with the story of the outrageous offerings at Hardee's and Carl's Jr. They were able to differentiate by creating unhealthy options for customers at the same time that other fast food chains like McDonald's were creating healthy options.

Now it looks like McDonald's is changing course. They aren't necessarily creating new high-calorie, high-fat items; they're just removing many of the more wholesome ones. According to the *Wall Street Journal* in March 2017, "McDonald's has decided to shift focus back to core products. After losing about 500 million US orders over the past five years over failed attempts to widen its customer base, the fast-food chain said it is going to embrace its identity as an affordable fast-food chain and stop chasing after people who will rarely eat there."[17]

A customer survey showed that they were losing customers to other fast food restaurants, not to outlets offering healthy foods. They also saw that their own healthy options weren't selling very well. In response, McDonald's is removing some of their low-calorie, low-fat menu items like oatmeal, wraps, and salads. Apparently, their customers are lopsided, and they need to be lopsided too.

Here are some additional examples of brands that are intentionally lopsided:

Velveeta strikes gold – The next Lopsiding example comes from the *Golden Goldfish* book in this series. Gold is based on the simple premise that all customers are not created equal. It advocates that paying attention to your top customers is a recipe for success. Joseph Juran, who coined the Pareto Principle, espoused the importance of taking care of your "vital few." He found that for the vast majority of businesses, 80 percent of profitability is generated by just 20 percent of customers.

---

17. https://www.wsj.com/articles/mcdonalds-to-expand-mobile-delivery-as-it-plots-future-1488390702

In the *Harvard Business Review* article, *"Make Your Best Customers Even Better,"* authors Eddie Yoon, Steve Carlotti, and Dennis Moore bring this to life with the example of Kraft Velveeta cheese.[18] In 2012, the Velveeta brand experienced its third consecutive year of declining sales. What could Kraft do to reverse this trend? Could they get new or lapsed customers to try the product? Could they get infrequent purchasers to buy the product more consistently?

The brand managers studied how the brand was being consumed. Research found the top 10 percent of Velveeta buyers account for over 50 percent of all sales of the product. And these consumers were not getting enough Velveeta in their lives. Kraft decided to focus on this key segment of 2.4 million consumers.

The results are anything but cheesy. New product spin-offs totaling over $100 million in additional sales in the next 18 months were a game changer. It has shifted a paradigm for Kraft. According to marketing director Greg Gallagher, "The previous thinking was that the quickest, easiest path to growth was to identify light users or lapsed users. But when we talked to superconsumers, we learned that in fact they wanted to use Velveeta more— they were starving for it."

All customers are not created equal. Lopsiding is doing more for your best ones. In the words of Yoon, Carlotti, and Moore, "Show the love to those that love you the most."

Sometimes a Pink Goldfish is also a Golden Goldfish and it's made of melted processed cheese.

Jeep transcends its flaws - "It handles like a 1967 school bus with an alignment issue." This quote is from Isaac Rogers describing his Jeep Wrangler. Isaac explains how the objectively worst car he's ever owned became his favorite vehicle. It taught him a valuable lesson about authentic brand experiences.

He continues, "If you were to measure a Jeep on generic 'industry benchmarks'- reliability, comfort, fuel economy...these are truly terrible cars." Yet, Rogers still loves the brand.

"I think I will own a Wrangler for the rest of my life. Why? Because it's stayed true to its authentic values. It doesn't try to be the best handling or the fastest or the most comfortable. Jeep realizes why people buy their cars, and it doubles down on those things and avoids chasing 'sameness.'"

Jeep is a great example of Lopsiding. Don't try to fix an imperfection. Double down on it. The Wrangler is one of the few remaining four-wheel-drives with solid front and rear axles. These axles are known for their durability, strength, and articulation, not for a smooth ride.

18. https://hbr.org/2014/03/make-your-best-customers-even-better

80 years ago, Willys-Overland demonstrated Jeep's off-road capability by driving it up the steps of the US Capitol. When asked by a columnist what it was called, the driver answered, "It's a jeep."

Sometimes a Pink Goldfish is bumpy and uncomfortable.

The Cheesecake Factory menu - When it comes to menu size, shouldn't you keep it simple? Don't paralyze customers with choice. Less is more right? Take for example In-N-Out Burger. Their entire menu has eight items. Or maybe not.

Boasting over 250 menu items, (including 85 different ways to order chicken and 50 different types of cheesecake) The Cheesecake Factory menu is nearly 6,000 words. Their notoriously massive menu consists of 21 oversized and spiral-bound pages.

What makes the lopsided menu even more impressive is that they are a scratch kitchen. Everything (other than the cheesecakes) is made fresh onsite. Prep begins at 6 a.m. with over 700 ingredients to make the 250 items. There are over 160 sauces made daily.

The lopsided size of the menu makes it remarkable. In the words of Jay Baer and Daniel Lemin in their book *Talk Triggers*,

> Because the vastness of the restaurant's menu is so unusual that it compels conversation among its patrons. Menu breadth is its secret customer-acquisition weapon—it hides in plain sight, in the hands of each and every diner. The menu at The Cheesecake Factory is a talk trigger: a built-in differentiator that creates customer conversations.

The Cheesecake Factory's lopsided menu leads to lopsided results. Their 220 restaurants earn almost $2.5 billion each year and they have a market capitalization of $2.67 billion. The menu has even made it to the silver screen. In the movie, *The Spy Who Dumped Me*, Audrey, played by Mila Kunis, tells Morgan that she and Drew went to The Cheesecake Factory, to which Morgan, played by Kate McKinnon, replies: "God, that menu. Too many options."

South of the Border - "You never sausage a place. You are always a wiener at Pedro's!" There are only 3 types of people in this world. Those that don't recognize this as a billboard for South of the Border . . . and those that can't count.

Growing up in New York, Stan can remember the long car rides to visit his Nana in St. Petersburg, Florida. As a 6-year-old, he can remember being bored out of his mind. These were the days before even a Walkman, let alone an iPod or a tablet.

Halfway on the journey down I-95 to the Sunshine State, the billboards would begin. Dozens of them. All counting down the miles to South of the Border.

Located just over the South Carolina border in Dillon, this flawsome attraction began in 1949. In response to the prohibition of alcohol sales in his North Carolina county, Alan Schafer opened a pink, cinder-block stand and named it South of the Border Beer Depot. A couple of years later a motel was added and the name was shortened to South of the Border.

Pedro, the star of each billboard, was born out of two motel employees from Mexico. Schafer had met them on a business trip. Customers collectively referred to both bellhops as Pedro.

If you haven't been, Libby Wiersema gives the best description, "If Las Vegas hooked up with Route 66 and had a baby, this would be it." To be clear, South of the Border is successful because they put almost all of their budget into billboard advertising and almost nothing into facilities or services. They don't try to be well-balanced or well-rounded. They definitely don't seem to be looking for referrals or repeat business. They are lopsided.

Sometimes a Pink Goldfish is a silly billboard.

PERSONAL BRANDING PROFILE

While in art school, Phil Hansen developed an uncontrollable shake in his hand due to his pointillism work. In his words, "It was actually good for some things, like mixing a can of paint or shaking a Polaroid, but at the time this was really doomsday. This was the destruction of my dream of becoming an artist."[19] Hansen dropped out and quit painting.

But after a few years, he just couldn't stay away from art. A trip to a neurologist revealed permanent nerve damage in his hand. His doctor looked at his squiggly lines and challenged Phil, "Well, why don't you just embrace the shake?"

He went home and let his hand shake when drawing. The result was scribbled pictures. It felt great for Hansen. He realized he just had to find a different approach to making the art that he wanted. Hansen began experimenting by dipping his feet in paint and walking on a canvas. He built a 3D structure consisting of two-by-fours and created a 2D image by burning it with a blowtorch.

Hansen began to understand that flaws could actually drive creativity. He pushed himself further and began to lopside his creativity. Some of his creations have included: using hundreds of live worms to make an image, using a pushpin to tattoo a banana, and painting a picture with hamburger grease.

Continued...

19. http://onwardmag.com/how-flaunting-your-weaknesses-can-build-trust/

Photo Credit: Stan Phelps and Phil Hansen at NSA Influence 2019

Want to learn more about Phil Hansen and his journey? Check out his 10-minute TED talk.[20] It has been viewed over two million times.

Sometimes a Pink Goldfish is embracing the shake.

20. https://www.ted.com/talks/phil_hansen_embrace_the_shake/transcript

PINK PROFILE

Pink is the only true rock and roll color.

- Paul Simonon of *The Clash*

The Clash was an iconic punk rock band and was part of a movement that went beyond music to become a subculture. Punk rock is a great example of Lopsiding. Punk is about more. More volume. Louder. More speed. Faster. More originality. Weirder. In a March 2017 article in *i-D* magazine, Alice Newell-Harrison described pink as "punk and pretty." So what is the connection between punk and pink? Why does Paul Simonon like pink so much?

Valerie Steele, in her book *Pink: The History of a Punk, Pretty, Powerful Color* explains that "punks reveled in 'bad taste.'" Pink was punk because the color was seen by many as "vulgar and tasteless." This is exactly what made it perfect for punks. "Pink appealed to a generation attracted to their artificiality and garishness." Punks took pink to a new level and then Kitten Kay Sera took it even farther.

Kitten Kay Sera has built her personal brand around pink. She has pink hair, pink clothes, a pink car, pink walls, pink appliances, and a pink dog. Everything is pink. She's been recognized in many publications as the pinkest person on Earth. Her apartment was featured on the *Netflix* series, *Amazing Interiors*, because it's so pink.

Her *Instagram* account, @kittenkaysera, has more than 169,000 followers. She's in commercials, advertisements, and television shows for no other reason than that she is really, really, pink. She makes money from simply being extraordinarily pink, ridiculously pink, and outrageously pink. She's gone farther than most people will go in their preference for a single color and that's what makes her unique.

Lopsiding is based on the belief that when people tell you that you've gone too far, maybe you haven't gone far enough, maybe you should go even farther, and get even pinker.

The L in F.L.A.W.S.O.M.E. framework is for Lopsiding, accentuating your flaws. Let's move on to the A...

CHAPTER 8

ANTAGONIZING

*"It doesn't matter how many people hate your brand
as long as enough people love it....
You can't be afraid of offending people.
You can't try and go down the middle of the road.
You have to take a stand on something."*

— Phil Knight, Founder of Nike

THE "A" IN F.L.A.W.S.O.M.E. STANDS FOR ANTAGONIZING

Antagonizing is about polarizing, alienating, repelling, and taunting. When most brands encounter irate customers, they try to soothe or placate or pacify or calm or reassure. They want to win over or win back the irate customer. They want to hug them and exceed their expectations. During planning sessions, they use focus groups and customer surveys. The goal is to discover what all people want and then give it to them. That's definitely not what we're recommending.

We want you to intentionally exasperate, irritate, provoke, aggravate, and instigate hostility. Go out of your way to rub some people the wrong way. Try to earn a few more one-star reviews on *Amazon* or *Yelp*. As Sally Hogshead, author of *Fascinate*, declares, "If you're not eliciting a negative response from someone, then you're probably not very compelling to anyone."

Tell your employees to increase the number of complaints. Make customer satisfaction less of a priority. Ring a bell in the office every time you get a nasty email. Try it. We promise, the more some people hate you, the more other people will love you.

Antagonizing occupies two sides of the flaunting zone. It is both the act of doing MORE of what makes you weak or imperfect and doing LESS of what is considered normal and perfect by others.

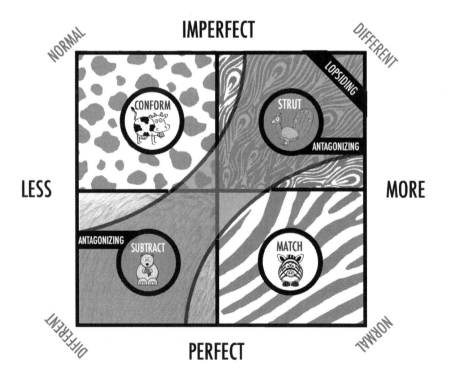

Here's a great example of Antagonizing:

Remember (not to text at) The Alamo - The Alamo Drafthouse Cinema was founded by Tim and Karrie League in 1998 in Austin, Texas. They have 50 locations across the United States, more than half of which are in Texas. Their strictly enforced policy of movie-going etiquette has made them both famous and infamous. They have clear rules that everyone has to follow. If someone breaks the rules, they are punished.

Many brands increasingly monitor the internet for negative product reviews and contact reviewers to remedy complaints, even going as far as to persuade customers to revise reviews with higher ratings. Not the Alamo Drafthouse Cinema; they take movie-going seriously. They are obsessed with the cinema experience, and they know their approach will make some people unhappy, and that it will make others very unhappy.

They maintain strict rules for both talking and texting during a movie, and for late arrivals. Additionally, children under two are not allowed in the theater except for special events. Unsupervised minors are not allowed either unless they are 15 years old and have been accepted into a membership program, which includes training on the theater's many policies. As you can see, they take this seriously. You have to take a class to be admitted into a movie theater.

Alamo knows that their approach isn't popular with everyone. Tim League posted this explanation on their website, "When we adopted our strict no talking policy back in 1997, we knew we were going to alienate some of our patrons. That was the plan. If you can't change your behavior and be quiet (or unilluminated) during a movie, then we don't want you at our venue."

Violators of the rules are given a warning and are then subject to removal. And they will remove you. One moviegoer found this out the hard way in 2011. And she did not take it well. It was so epic that Alamo turned it into a Public Service Announcement that they show before the movie starts. Here's the transcript:

> **Alamo Drafthouse:** *At the Alamo Drafthouse, we have a simple rule: If you talk or text during a movie, we kick you out. Sometimes, that pisses the movie talker off. What follows is an actual voicemail a customer left us after being kicked out.*
>
> **Customer:** Yeah, I was wondering if you guys actually enjoy treating your customers like pieces of sh*t? Because that's how I felt when I went to the Alamo Drafthouse.
>
> Okay? You know what? I didn't know that I wasn't supposed to text in your little crappy ass theater. It was too f*cking dark in that place to even find my seat. All right? I was using my phone as a flashlight to get to my f*ckin' seat.

So excuse me for using my phone in USA Magnited States of America, where you are free to text in a theater. I was not aware that I couldn't text in your theater. All right?

I've texted in all the other theaters in Austin. And no one ever gave a f*ck about what me, I was doing with my f*ckin' phone. All right? And it was on silent. It wasn't on loud. It wasn't bothering anybody.

You guys obviously were being assh*les to me. And I'm sure that's what you do. You know, to rip people off. You take my money and you throw me out. You know?

I will never be comin' back to your Alamo Drafthouse or whatever. I'd rather go to a regularlier theater where people are actually polite. You know?

I'm gonna tell everyone about how sh*tty you are. And I'm pretty sure you guys are being assh*les on purpose. So thanks for making me feel like a customer. Thanks for takin' my money, assh*le!

Alamo Drafthouse: You're welcome! Thanks for not coming back to the Alamo, texter!

League is unapologetic. "We wanted to take a hard stand and say that those people are not welcome at the Alamo Drafthouse. So [we] will get rid of those people and just make it a better place for the rest of the movie-going public."

By the way, the "Don't Talk PSA | Angry Voicemail" also went viral outside of the theater. The video has garnered over 4.5 million views on *YouTube* and was featured by Anderson Cooper on *CNN*.

Alamo prides itself as a cinema built by movie fans for movie fans. They purposely embraced this complaint to emphasize how serious they are about movies. They've done more of what makes them weird as a business. If you don't like it, you can leave. If they don't like you, they'll make you leave. If you complain, they'll put you on the big screen.

Sometimes a Pink Goldfish is a list of strictly enforced rules.

Let's look at some more companies that antagonize customers:

OMG! WTF? BVG - I (David) was speaking at a conference for entrepreneurs in November 2018 in Barcelona. The audience was mostly from Europe and I presented *Pink Goldfish*. It was one of the first times I'd done the presentation and the first time sharing it with an international audience. I wasn't sure if the concept would translate well, especially since many of the examples were from North America. But it went really well.

I was having lunch with some of the participants and a guy from Germany shared a fantastic example from Berlin. He didn't know a lot of the specific details, but he said that BVG (Berliner Verkehrsbetriebe) definitely antagonized their customers.

I looked into it and, unfortunately, most of the information about them was in German. But I found an article on *Medium.com* by Rumen Manev from February 2018.[21] He explains that "one of the things that distinguishes the BVG is the brand identity they've built through the years and the unusual way they engage with their audience."

Engaging is an interesting way to describe their interactions with riders. Attacking might be a better description. Maybe harassing. Definitely provoking and alienating.

BVG is responsible for the subway, trams, busses, and ferries in Berlin, a diverse German city of four million people. They serve more than a billion riders each year. As you can imagine, there are a lot of problems and inconveniences in such a large transportation system. These, in turn, lead to a lot of complaints.

When BVG started a new ad campaign, they chose the slogan "Because we love you." To most Berliners, this was ludicrous. It sure didn't seem like BVG loved its customers. They took to social media every day to remind BVG just how unloved they felt.

Most organizations would respond to this negative public onslaught in two ways. First, end the "because we love you" campaign. Write it off as a mistake and come up with something new. Second, start trying to respond to individual complaints and make necessary improvements to improve customer satisfaction.

But that's not what BVG did. They defended their campaign and went on the offensive. They didn't apologize. They didn't try to resolve the complaints. They attacked the complainers.

They hired two comedy writers to take over their social media and began a series of ad campaigns that flaunted the negative aspects of the riding experience. "Unconditional self-irony" is how Manev describes their strategy.

> Instead of ignoring what people were complaining about, especially the things that were beyond the power of the administration, the voices of the BVG started making jokes about it. Their idea was to create a brand around the chaotic, smelly, trashy environment that is the public transport system. It's the perfect reflection of what the actual city is about. Berlin can be dirty, messy and rough, but this is exactly what grew

---

21. https://room-n.medium.com/the-case-of-the-berlin-public-transport-6162f1be65b6

to be its charm. In a way, the BVG perfectly captures what Berlin is about —sure, it has its issues, but that's what makes it so special.

The BVG public voice is humorous and somewhat unapologetic. . . . people who address the BVG often get a response fairly quickly, albeit a response that usually makes a joke out of them.

For example, Julian Bolter complained on *Twitter* about the uncomfortable seats with this sarcastic tweet.

"Composition of the new subway seats: 20% fabric and 80% hard plastic. Very comfortable!"

BVG replied with empathy and compassion (read this sarcastically).

"That way our seats have the same composition as the Kardashians."

No apology. No promise of improvement. Just antagonizing.

There are a couple issues here. First, public transportation will always be somewhat unpleasant, precisely because it is public. People will always have complaints, no matter how well BVG performs. Second, BVG is not able to fix the majority of the issues people complain about. Instead of apologizing, and pretending that they can magically make everyone happy, they manage their riders' expectations by sarcastically responding to feedback. They refuse to legitimize the complaint.

It might seem like this antagonistic approach would increase the negative comments on social media, but their response has actually decreased the negativity. People are learning that BVG either can't or won't address their concerns, so why bother complaining. Furthermore, a complaint opens the complainer up to public humiliation when BVG's social media team roasts them online.

We'll talk about alignment in a later chapter, but this quote from Manev seems especially relevant. Berlin is "the perfect place for a sarcastic... public transport to thrive." This approach might not work everywhere, but it works in Berlin. Maybe it will work for you.

One additional note: While researching BVG, we found a lot of their antagonistic responses to complaints on social media. When we translated them, we discovered that they were much too obscene and vulgar to share in the book. Let's just say that BVG is in the Antagonizing hall of fame. If you aren't easily offended, look them up online.

Sometimes a Pink Goldfish is a dirty subway.

Dick's Last Resort trains servers to be obnoxious – Dick's Last Resort was founded by Dick Chase in 1985. Chase had formerly gone bankrupt while trying to run an upscale fine dining restaurant. He decided to "go sloppy" on his second effort and developed a completely different approach. Dick's tagline is "socially unacceptable," which is a great example of flaunting. They are unapologetic.

Instead of training their servers to be polite and helpful, they teach them to be rude and obnoxious. They are insulting and intentionally provide customers with bad service. For example, napkins aren't placed on the table. If someone wants a napkin, one is thrown at them.

Servers aren't the only thing that is rude at Dick's. They encourage people to post #dickspicks and #dickmove on social media. They sell offensive T-shirts and bumper stickers proclaiming that "Real Women Love Dick's" and "I Love Dick's." Their tasteless menu includes the "Dolly Parton: a voluptuously grilled chicky breast."

Dick's isn't the only restaurant to succeed with this antagonistic model.

Ed Debevic's opened in 1984 in Chicago. It's a 1950's themed diner with burgers, fries, shakes, and really rude servers, who have to audition in order to get the job. A video of one of their mean servers, Kryssie "Cherry" Ridolfi, went viral in 2015 and has more than 4 million views on social media. They also sell the "world's smallest sundae." After closing for a few years, Ed's is reopening in 2020, although that has been delayed because of the COVID-19 pandemic.

Similarly, Ben Baker told us about The Elbow Room Cafe in Vancouver. It was founded in 1983 by Bryan Searle and Patrick Savoie, and is famous for their snarky, cheeky, and sassy service. Their menu proclaims to customers that "food and service is our name, abuse is our game!" They also offer items such as "Big Ass Pancakes" and "I Have No Imagination" omelets.

The restaurant is so legendary, that Dave Deveau and Anton Lipovetsky wrote a play about it. In 2017, *Elbow Room Cafe: The Musical* debuted at the York Theatre. Not many diners are unique enough to inspire this kind of attention and affection.

Sometimes a Pink Goldfish is rude service . . . and a musical.

Instagram post: "Have you seen this account? She takes real one-star reviews from national parks and illustrates them."

"She" refers to Raleigh based Amber Share and her *Instagram* account @subparparks.

For example, Amber illustrates a one-star review about the Grand Canyon below. "A HOLE. A VERY, VERY LARGE HOLE."

The *Instagram* account has over 300,000 followers. Here are some of our favorites:

- For Hawai'i Volcanoes National Park, "DIDN'T EVEN GET TO TOUCH THE LAVA"

- For Bryce Canyon National Park, "TOO ORANGE, TOO SPIKY"

According to an interview in *Midwest Living*, Amber created the account as a "snarky love letter" to the National Parks System. In her words, "When I discovered that there were 1-star reviews for every single one of the 62 national parks, I set out to illustrate each park along with a hand-lettered 1-star review as a way to put a positive, fun spin on such a negative mindset."

Takeaway: Some people (and evidently some National Parks) are A HOLE. If you try to please everyone, you please no one. Why not have a little fun with the haters? Who is in your anti-target market?

Five Guys doesn't care about your peanut allergy - If you need to fly and you have a peanut allergy, the airline will try to protect you. They won't give out peanuts on your flight. They'll also make an announcement to request that people don't consume any peanut products on the plane.

If you want a burger and you have a peanut allergy, Five Guys Burger and Fries won't do anything to protect you. They fry everything in peanut oil, there are piles of peanuts stacked everywhere, and they leave peanut shells all over the floor. If a person with a peanut allergy goes into Five Guys, they might be risking their life.

As you can imagine, this leads to a lot of questions and complaints. Here is how Five Guys responds on their website:

> If so many people are allergic to peanuts, why does Five Guys continue to offer them? Over the last 20 years, peanuts have become part of the Five Guys identity. We by no means want to exclude guests from our store, but at the same time we would not want to disappoint our peanut-eating guests. We make sure that we have signage on our doors and in our restaurants about the fact that we serve peanuts in bulk containers as we would never want someone to risk their health by coming into our restaurants.

I'm not sure if it's possible to be more antagonizing than this. It is one thing for a product or service to make potential customers unhappy. It is another thing for a product or service to physically harm or kill potential customers.

Five Guys isn't even selling peanuts. They give them away. It costs them millions of dollars a year to provide peanuts for free to every customer, but they won't stop. They know that their peanuts threaten people's health, but they refuse to remove them because they are such an important part of their brand identity.

It seems like this approach would cause some kind of backlash and would limit the company's success, but it hasn't. Five Guys is looking to double their number of locations in the coming years. President Barack Obama is a big fan and so are a lot of other customers. Five Guys has won the award for Best Burger from *Zagat*. They were also ranked #1 in a Market Force survey on food quality, taste, service, cleanliness, and atmosphere, and they've been the top burger brand two years in a row in a Harris Poll survey.

Sometimes a Pink Goldfish causes an allergic reaction.

Shinesty is unapologetically not sorry - Familiar with the *Shinesty* catalog? *Shinesty* is a Boulder-based e-commerce company co-founded in 2014 by Chris White, Jens Nicolaysen, and Michelle Frey-Tarbox. They have a simple mission:

To bring you the most outlandish collection of clothing the world has ever seen.

When worn correctly, the right clothing can make Mike Tyson's albino tiger purr like a kitten, blow the minds of boringly-dressed onlookers, or be a major contributing factor in the creation of a small human that looks strikingly similar to you.

Whether you are searching for a rare retro piece, enough neon to blind the 80s, or simply something that would make Chuck Norris weep with pride, Shinesty is here to help.

Stay Weird & Shine On

Shinesty prides itself on its eye-grabbing holiday catalog. One might say that some of the material is risqué. It has spawned a number of complaints. Shinesty addressed this in a blogpost entitled, "We owe you all an apology for our Holiday catalog."

We're Sorry...

November 16, 2018 · Entertainment, Holidays, Humor

We owe you all an apology for our Holiday catalog.

We get it, some of you are upset about having a few pieces of paper sent to your mailbox.

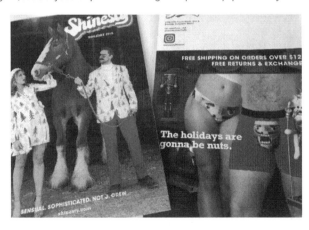

The post by Austin Rosmarin begins, "We get it, some of you are upset about having a few pieces of paper sent to your mailbox." It then shares commentary on a number of complaints.

Here's an example:

We don't need a publicist to know a crisis like this requires a swift, heartfelt apology.

Naturally, we took a page right out of BP's playbook.

Founder Jens Nicolaysen replied, "We'll save what would have been your copies in a heap in our office JUSTIN CASE you change your mind."

Shinesty's antagonistic approach is paying off. They have an impressive revenue per employee of $228,000. Surprisingly, they also recently won second place in the Effortless Experience Customer Happiness Awards. This demonstrates the primary lesson of Antagonizing. As much as some people might hate your company, others will love it even more.

Sometimes a Pink Goldfish is outlandish, cheeky, and unapologetic.

Nike gets burned, literally - In September 2018, Nike released an incredibly controversial advertising campaign featuring Colin Kaepernick, the former NFL quarterback, who was revered and reviled for taking a knee during the national anthem before football games. He was protesting police brutality and the killing of unarmed black citizens. Kaepernick's actions made him extremely unpopular with many football fans and may have led to his inability to find a team willing to hire him as their quarterback.

In the ads, Nike's tagline was printed over either a video of Kaepernick or his photo, depending on the medium.

**Believe in something,
even if it means
sacrificing everything.**

The response from critics and citizens was immediate and extreme on social media and in traditional media. People were talking about it, but they were also taking action.

Nike was criticized for a lack of patriotism and for not supporting the police and the military. They were also praised for supporting equal rights and fighting against racial inequality.

Some people predicted the end of Nike, a loss of sales and stock value.
People burned their shoes and jerseys.

Other people predicted the resurgence of Nike, a rise in sales and stock price.
People bought their shoes and jerseys.

Nike was held up as an example of a brand who had just made a colossal mistake.

Nike was used as an example of a brand who had just made a brilliant move.

Everyone had an opinion. Everyone cared. No one was neutral.

Phil Knight, Nike's founder, explained it this way. "It doesn't matter how many people hate your brand as long as enough people love it. And as long as you have that attitude, you can't be afraid of offending people. You can't try and go down the middle of the road. You have to take a stand on something, which is ultimately why the Kaepernick ad worked."

And it did seem to work. Nike's stock was worth $82.20 per share before the ad campaign on August 31, 2018. Since then, they've seen a 59 percent increase in stock value. As of October 9, 2020, Nike's stock was worth $130.98 per share.

Additionally, the societal reaction to Nike's stance has also changed substantially. It is now common for professional basketball, baseball, and football games to be postponed in protest of police shootings or other instances of injustice. In 2020 the NBA allowed players to display messages of equality or social justice on their uniforms. The NFL did something similar on the backs of players' helmets. More notably, players across the country, in amateur and professional sports, are kneeling during the national anthem with much more widespread support from coaches, families, and communities. It seems that Nike, just like Kaepernick, was a little ahead of their time and maybe they paved the way for recent changes in society's attitudes and beliefs.

Sometimes a Pink Goldfish is not afraid to take a stance and offend.

dbrand alienates people on every platform - dbrand is a manufacturer of vinyl skins and wraps for mobile phones, tablets, laptops, and video game consoles. In their *Twitter* profile, they call their products "overpriced electronic tape that looks cool."

In a *Medium* post, Evan LaVigne explained that "their tone is very sassy and sometimes harsh... and their humor is crass." He went on to describe their communication as "savage" and "insensitive." We think that is an understatement.

Here is a sampling of their abuse from nearly every digital channel.

They antagonize customers on *Twitter*. When they refunded Sony PlayStation 5 skin pre-orders, they said it was because "you idiots can't install them correctly." This might seem playful, but they use the same approach in apparently serious situations as well. For example, it is likely that dbrand will be sued by Sony for making PlayStation 5 faceplates. When they were asked about this possibility, dbrand said "we encourage them to try."

They antagonize via email. This isn't a traditional corporate sales or marketing email:

> You think too much. If morons like you spent less time thinking and more time mindlessly buying things, we could use the proceeds from this drop for something other

than advancing the scientific field of human lobotomies. Now, buy stuff like your brain depends on it.

They antagonize on their website. This is an ad for their new facemask:

Wear a mask. School is back in session. The government doesn't care whether you live or die. To be fair, neither do we. We do, however, care about monetizing your face.

Their *Google* AdSense copy gets straight to the point:

In about 10 minutes, we'll have your money, stop wasting our time.

They make no attempt to convince or persuade. For example, this is how they announced a recent sale on their website:

We're having a 20% sale sitewide. What's the occasion? We launched brand new Matte Black Switch skins and tempered glass. You don't own a switch, so it doesn't matter or maybe you do and you just haven't bought anything for it yet. Why is that? Who hurt you? Again, it doesn't matter.

The time has come for you to empty your bank account . . . into ours. It's time to buy skins for every device you own. Stick them to tables. Cover a window to block all natural light. Construct an elaborate mask out of vinyl skins - nobody wanted to see your face anyway. Buy now or be stuck with our exorbitant non-sale prices forever.

There are so many examples of dbrand's relentless assaults on everyone they interact with that we can't possibly share them all here. This isn't a fleeting campaign or a temporary approach that they're testing. Antagonizing is their identity.

Here is one more of our favorites from Black Friday.

Let's face it. Black Friday sucks. Every year, the human race decides to collectively embarrass themselves on some arbitrary Friday in November. The crowds are huge, the lines are long, and riots triggered by sold-out PlayStations are inevitable. The entire event is nothing more than a recurring tribute to hollow, meaningless consumerism.

Our Matte Black Friday promotion is a little different. Don't get us wrong - the hollow, meaningless consumerism is still there. We simply added a word and roped in a massively successful YouTuber who has a strange obsession with Matte Black.

As an added bonus, there are no discounts. Welcome to 2020.

Antagonizing works. It's possible that dbrand is more famous for their social media harassment than they are for their actual products. People can't stop talking about, and sharing, dbrand's outrageous posts and replies. In doing so, they are spreading the word about dbrand's products as well. dbrand succeeds by monetizing mean marketing.

Sometimes a Pink Goldfish is a needlessly cruel and condescending sales pitch.

PERSONAL BRANDING PROFILE

Elon Musk loves to antagonize. He's rarely without a nemesis and has no problem speaking his mind. Elon recently took a swipe at CEOs. "There's the M.B.A.-ization of America, which I think is maybe not that great. There should be more focus on the product or service itself, less time on board meetings, less time on financials."

Musk made the comments during *The Wall Street Journal's* CEO Council Summit. He went further, "I think there might be too many M.B.A.s running companies."

The degree isn't really the issue. The issue is that Musk feels that today's executives are too focused on spreadsheets and powerpoints. They need to get out of the boardroom and spend more time on the factory floor. The Japanese call it the Gemba. The Gemba is an opportunity for executives to step away and walk the floor of their workplace. The objective of Gemba Walk is to understand the value stream and its problems rather than just results.

When Musk isn't making generalizations, he's quick to "beef" with his fellow industry titans. *NY Magazine* chronicled his fight with Jeff Bezos:[22]

> This battle of the billionaires was fought over a dormant NASA space pad at the Kennedy Space Center. Musk wanted it for SpaceX, Bezos wanted it for Blue Origin, and they each had different ideas on how to run it. What could have been a simple competition for infrastructure turned into a full-on beef when Musk said the odds of Blue Origin launching a suborbital spacecraft in the next five years were lower than "discovering unicorns dancing in the flame duct." Ouch.

22. https://nymag.com/intelligencer/2014/03/elon-musks-got-beef-a-time-line.html

PINK PROFILE

Why would anyone pick blue over pink?
Pink is obviously a better color.

— Kanye West

Pink is an antagonizing color. In a French study, only two percent of respondents chose pink as their favorite color while 17 percent chose pink as their least favorite color. Only brown was less popular than pink. There are even those who go so far as to argue that pink isn't even a real color.

Barbara Nemitz, author of *Pink: The Exposed Color in Contemporary Culture*, suggests that "many people have little regard for pink." She goes on to describe the "polarizing effect of pink."

> What is unique about pink is that it is assertive in whatever context it appears. Pink is the way it is and it makes no attempts to disguise itself. It is vulnerable to attack, and it tends to polarize. Its increasing popularity as a modern color in recent years may be attributable to its challenging and complicated qualities.

Valerie Steele agrees. In *Pink: The History of a Punk, Pretty, Powerful Color,* she argues that "pink provokes exceptionally strong feelings of both attraction and repulsion." It is a color that is both "glorified and denigrated." Steele goes on to describe pink as the "most divisive" and the "most controversial" color.

People hate pink and they love it. They think it's the worst and the best, awful and amazing, ugly and beautiful, weak and strong, imperfect and perfect. As Nemitz explains, "the scale of social attitudes toward pink runs to extremes."

The A in F.L.A.W.S.O.M.E. is for Antagonizing, being polarizing. Let's move on to the W...

CHAPTER 9

WITHHOLDING

"Sometimes saying no is the best way to get customers to say yes."

— Will Burns, *Forbes*

THE W IN F.L.A.W.S.O.M.E. STANDS FOR WITHHOLDING

Most brands are trying to be strong, and they want to get stronger. They want to be powerful. This seems to make sense. Be the best. Do more. Expand. Grow. Offer more features, more products, more services, and more locations. But maybe there's a better way.

Withholding is about limitations, restrictions, boundaries, and constraints. That sounds obviously negative. Don't great brands offer freedom? Don't customers want services to be unlimited? Shouldn't the best organizations be everywhere all the time? Even if we don't serve everyone, we certainly want more customers, don't we?

Lopsiding is about doing more of what makes you weak and weird, not more of what everyone else is doing. This chapter is all about doing LESS, but not less of what makes you weak and weird. Instead, we want you to do less of what makes other brands normal and strong.

Withholding involves offering fewer options, fewer locations, fewer features, fewer products, fewer services, fewer hours, fewer perks, and fewer discounts. Avoiding is deliberately and relentlessly shrinking the things that everyone else is expanding.

Withholding sits at the opposite end of the matrix from Lopsiding.

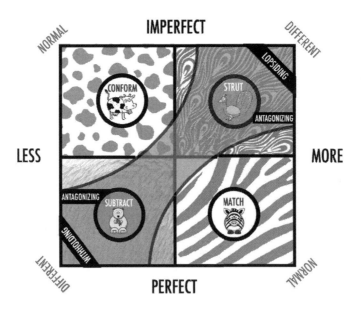

It is doing LESS of what is considered normal or good by others. By reducing options or completely eliminating them, brands can stand out and differentiate themselves.

Withholding can help us succeed and stand out. In *The Paradox of Choice*, Barry Schwartz explains that when we have too many choices, we struggle to make decisions. He encourages us to "learn to love constraints" because "as the number of choices we face increases, freedom of choice becomes a tyranny of choice. Routine decisions take so much time and attention that it becomes difficult to get through the day. In circumstances like this, we should learn to view limits on the possibilities that we face as liberating not constraining."

Perhaps surprisingly, providing more options to customers can often paralyze them. As Erich Fromm explained in *Escape from Freedom*, "People are beset not by a lack of opportunity but by a dizzying abundance of it." It is counterintuitive, but limitations, not options, are what liberate customers.

Similarly, behavioral economist Dan Ariely, in *Predictably Irrational*, argues that the common strategy of "keeping our options open" is a bad one and that we should "consciously start closing" some of those options. This is true because "they draw energy and commitment" away from activities that promise greater success.

One of the most common brand goals is growth. Get bigger. Make more money, open more locations, hire more employees, and increase sales. But some brands deliberately shrink or maintain their small size. They resist the pressure to expand. They stay small on purpose.

Westvleteren Brewery doesn't want you to buy their beer - A great, and very unusual, example of Withholding is Westvleteren Brewery. The brewery was founded in 1838 and operates completely within the St. Sixtus Trappist Abbey in Vleteren, Belgium. Five monks manage the brewing process and five monks take care of the bottling. The goals of the brewery are simple, to provide meaningful work for the monks and to generate enough money to pay for the ongoing expenses at the abbey. Nothing more and nothing less.

Let's start with a list of all the things they don't do.

- No labels on the bottles
- No marketing or advertising
- No wholesale distribution (only sold to individual buyers)
- No bulk orders (maximum of two cases per person)
- No production increases since 1946
- No interviews (except to warn about reselling the beer)
- No regular business hours
- No participation in contests that compare beers
- No deliveries (all beer is picked up from the abbey)

That's a long list. So what are they doing? They brew three beers for only 72 days each year.

- Westvleteren 12
- Westvleteren 8
- Westvleteren Blonde

Before 2019, when all sales moved to their website, they would answer the phone for four hours on just two days each week. Phone reservations were required in order to purchase the beer. Voicemail was not an option. If you wanted the beer, you had to keep calling for hours until someone finally answered.

The beer is sold for just 36 days each year until the limited supply runs out. Each individual is restricted to one order (of 1-2 cases) every sixty days per phone number and license plate number. To be clear, this means that the only legitimate way for you to get their beer is to travel to Belgium to pick it up yourself.

At this point, you might be wondering why anyone would go through all this trouble for some weird religious beer. That is a great question and there is a very surprising answer. Westvleteren Brewery makes the best beer in the world. That isn't hyperbole. It's not an exaggeration. It's not marketing. Remember, they don't do marketing. It's just a fact.

In 2014, Westvleteren 12 was named the best beer in the world on *ratebeer.com*. A 2020 search on *ratebeer.com* shows a perfect rating of 100/100. Westvleteren 8 and Westvleteren 12 were ranked #2 and #3 on a 2011 list of the top 100 beers in Belgium. Westvleteren Blonde was in the top 25 on that same list.

Their beers are so popular that there is a very active black market, especially for Westvleteren 12. Beer lovers, as well as bars and pubs, around the world are desperate to get even a few bottles.

If all of this sounds confusing, that's because it is. According to their *Wikipedia* page, their practices "go against all modern business methods." That isn't accidental. As Father Abbott, a St. Sixtus monk, explains, "we are not brewers. We are monks. We brew beer to be able to afford being monks."

They are unapologetic. They are unashamed. They don't brew beer to please customers or win contests or make money. They brew beer in order to sustain their unusual way of life, to make it possible for them to practice their religious beliefs.

Westvleteren's unwillingness to expand is very unusual, but it isn't unprecedented.

Sometimes a Pink Goldfish won't sell you a beer.

Withholding isn't just about size. You can do less in almost any area of your business. Let's look at some additional examples.

Chick-fil-A refuses to open their restaurants – 7-Eleven takes its name from its original every day operating hours. The company pioneered the convenience store concept, capitalizing on the fact that most grocery stores were closed on Sundays. In the next 25 years, most retail establishments, including restaurants, followed suit and are now open seven-days a week with longer hours. Many are even open on major holidays like Thanksgiving.

Chick-fil-A bucks this trend. The restaurant is primarily known for being a mall-based fast-food chain. They first opened in Hapeville, Georgia, in 1946. Chick-fil-A's late founder, Truett Cathy made the conscious decision to be closed on Sundays.

According to *QPolitical*, the reason was practical as much as it was spiritually based. "Not only do they close on Sunday so believers can worship, they also want to make sure that [employees] have time to spend with [their] family. Not many companies care that much about their employees and it's refreshing to see one that truly does care."[23] The simple act of being closed on Sunday has become a true differentiator for the brand.

Chick-fil-A is so popular, especially in the South, that they've been the subject of adoring songs, videos, and comedy routines created by raving fans. Their chicken, lemonade, and sweet tea are a religion and an addiction for many customers. Many people simply can't live without Chick-fil-A. It would seem then that the company is leaving a lot of money on the table by refusing to add Sunday hours.

Their commitment to Withholding was tested on Sunday, February 3, 2019 when Super Bowl LIII was played at Mercedes-Benz Stadium in Atlanta, Georgia, which is also the location of the Chick-fil-A corporate headquarters. There is a Chick-fil-A location inside of the new stadium, which was just opened in late 2017. Imagine how many chicken sandwiches they would sell at Chick-fil-A in Mercedes-Benz Stadium in Atlanta on Super Bowl Sunday.

You don't have to imagine. They didn't sell any chicken sandwiches or any sweet tea or any lemonade. They stayed closed all day on Super Bowl Sunday in Atlanta when 70,000 football fans were there for several hours. That's the essence of Withholding.

Every other fast food chain is open seven days a week. Chick-fil-A is only open for six days a week. They're closed for 52 days per year, which means they are open 14.2 percent less than their competitors. Experts calculate that being closed on Sundays costs the company more than $1 billion per year in lost sales, especially because weekends often account for a larger share of fast food sales.

---

23. http://www.qpolitical.com/real-reason-chick-fil-closes-sunday-will-blow-mind/

Isn't this a huge disadvantage? Wouldn't they be more successful if they were open on Sundays? There's no way to know for sure.

However, in 2012 Chick-fil-A had the highest sales per store of any fast food chain at $3.1 million per store. In 2013, their total sales moved past KFC. In 2017, Chick-fil-A earned more per unit than McDonald's, Starbucks, and Subway combined. They had the highest growth of any fast food chain in 2018. As of 2019, they are the third-largest fast food chain with per unit sales that double that of McDonald's.

There's an old saying that "absence makes the heart grow fonder." Maybe Chick-fil-A builds up some anticipation, and desperation, and a sense of urgency by being closed on Sunday. It would be interesting to see if their Monday morning sales spike due to pent up demand. Regardless, it's clear, from the success of Chick-fil-A, that Withholding works.

Sometimes a Pink Goldfish doesn't go to work on Sunday.

> Chick-fil-A rejects 99.87 percent of all franchise applications. Out of 60,000 requests each year, only 80 are selected to operate a store. Does this restrictive approach work? It does. They have a 96 percent retention rate among their franchisees.

Lululemon sizing – Lululemon Athletica was founded in Vancouver, British Columbia, by Chip Wilson in 1998. Although they offer a wide range of high-end athletic apparel for men and women, they are most famous for their women's yoga pants that cost just under $100.

It is relatively common for clothing retailers to offer options for a wide range of shapes and sizes. In contrast, Lululemon made a strategic decision in 2013 that they wouldn't sell plus-size clothing. Specifically, they would only offer yoga pants in size 12 and under. This was a very controversial decision that was widely covered in the media and has made them very unpopular with some customers and consumer advocacy groups (Antagonizing). Despite this criticism, they've maintained the policy. During a 2018 search of their website, we were unable to find any athletic pants above size 12 available. In some instances, a size 14 was listed, but was "sold out online."

Lululemon explained their reasoning this way. "Our product and design strategy is built around creating products for our target guest in our size range of 2-12. While we know that doesn't work for everyone and recognize fitness and health come in all shapes and sizes, we've built our business, brand, and relationship with our guests on this formula."[24]

They acknowledge that their strategy limits the range of customers they can serve, and they are comfortable with that. "We want to be excellent at what we do, so this means that we can't be everything to everybody and need to focus on specific areas."

It is important to note the overlap here between Withholding and Antagonizing. Lululemon's limited sizing definitely makes customers and critics upset. They've experienced a lot of criticism because of this decision. It is very common to get negative feedback when your company chooses not to do something. If you're going to withhold, be ready to deal with complaints.

However, Lululemon's focus on little pants has paid big dividends. They had an almost 100 percent increase in their stock price in 2019 and they also won Forbes' Retailer of the Year Award. Revenue increased 11 percent to $4.4 billion in 2020, and they are predicting revenue growth of more than $1 billion in 2021.

Sometimes a Pink Goldfish gets so big that it can't buy pants from Lululemon.

Update: During the pandemic, Lululemon announced that they are now selling bigger sizes. It remains to be seen how this decision will affect their brand. However, it definitely opens the door for other brands in their industry to execute a Withholding strategy. This is exactly what Brandy Melville is doing.

Brandy Melville and "one-size-fits-most" - The apparel brand Brandy Melville takes Lululemon's strategy even farther. They only carry one size for the majority of their items. And that size is "S" as in small. Their clothes are tailored to a 25 inch waist and a 32 inch bust. These measurements are not representative of the vast majority of female consumers.

Started in the 1980s, the brand was inspired by the fictional tale of two people – Brandy, an American girl, and Melville, an English man who met in Rome and fell in love. Mark Villalovos pointed out their Withholding strategy to us, "They exclude a massive segment of the population and have been accused of fat shaming, but their popularity continues to gain a global following."

The Italian brand opened a store in Shanghai in 2019 and has since gained a large following among young women in China. Searches for the term "BM style" have exploded on the internet. In 2020, a series of videos appeared on *Douyin*, a Chinese app similar to *TikTok*. They showed young women weighing themselves and breathlessly calculating when they would lose enough weight to fit into the brand's crop tops and 24-inch jeans.

Sometimes a Pink Goldfish is one size fits (sm)all.

---

24. https://www.huffingtonpost.com/2013/08/02/lululemon-plus-size-clothing_n_3696690.html

Bob Ross helped pioneer a concept called "wet on wet" painting to the masses. You didn't need years of training. Bob believed everyone was an artist. Within 26 minutes, Ross would go from a blank canvas to a completed work.

His show *The Joy of Painting* on *PBS* made him a household name. His weird perm and beard made him unforgettable. Ross passed away in 1995, but he is still a popular figure today. He has nearly 4.7 million *YouTube* subscribers.

You'd think that people would collect Bob Ross paintings? You'd be wrong.

In a classic example of Withholding, you can't buy a Bob Ross painting. Over 1,000 of his landscapes from the show (he did 3 per episode) are located in Herndon, Virginia. They are not for sale, but you can buy paint, books, and other collectibles from *BobRoss.com*.

There is one exception. In 2019, the Smithsonian acquired many of his paintings for its permanent collection. Call it a happy little accident.

In-N-Out Burger won't add new items – Harry and Esther Snyder opened the first In-N-Out Burger in California in 1948. They currently have more than 350 locations along the West coast, and their fans are absolutely obsessed.

One thing that makes In-N-Out unique is their intentionally limited menu. It looks like something from the 1950s, and it is. The menu hasn't changed much in the last 70 years. There are just four basic options: burgers, fries, shakes, and fountain drinks. They don't offer chicken or fish or onion rings or kid's meals or cookies or breakfast or many of the other items you can get from most fast food chains.

Another way they withhold is with information. They have a secret menu of foods and options you can order that aren't on the official menu. For example, you can order up to four burger patties and four slices of cheese. It used to be unlimited until the late Tony Hsieh and his friends in Las Vegas ordered 100 patties and 100 slices of cheese, and ruined it for the rest of us.

You can also get your burger and/or fries "animal style," which includes specially grilled patties, extra sauce, and extra pickles. When you arrive at In-N-Out for the first time, it's unlikely you would know about these choices.

In-N-Out's unusually short menu is beneficial in a couple ways. It enables them to provide very fast service because they don't have to make a wide variety of foods. Also, their food is good because they do a few things really well. They are focused. Additionally, their secret menu gets people talking because it's fun to share a secret.

If you haven't heard of In-N-Out, it's probably because they are only located in California and are slowly expanding into a few other states in the Western US. Recent grand openings in Colorado saw wait times of 12-14 hours. This scarcity just makes them even more popular with their fans.

Sometimes a Pink Goldfish sandwich isn't on the menu.

Tofino Distillery takes traditional to heart - Tofino is a distillery based in the British Columbia town of the same name. Situated on Victoria Island, this Canadian brand is committed to creating traditionally handcrafted premium quality vodkas and gins. Founded in June 2018 by local volunteer firefighters Adam Warry, John Gilmour, and Neil Campbell, the trio prides themselves on producing certified organic spirits. Deanne Topping pointed out to us how they've leveraged Withholding. According to their website,

> In an effort to preserve our traditional approach, *we have opted not to brand with social media*. In lieu of this, we hope to provide a more intimate, personal experience for all. Please visit us in person or email us at the link provided below. We would love to hear from you.

Jimmy John's gets freaky – If you want a sub sandwich delivered freaky fresh and freaky fast, you should call Jimmy John's. They promise to deliver it to you in five minutes or less. So how do they do it?

There are two parts to their speed strategy. First, they only make cold subs. These can be made more quickly because they don't require heating or cooking. Second, they have a very limited delivery radius. In some places, it is less than two miles.

This narrow service range allows them to fulfill their promise of freaky fast and fresh delivery. However, it leaves a lot of people out. If you're not in the zone, you can't get your sandwich delivered. If they can't do it in five minutes or less, they don't do it at all.

They flaunt this limitation in a 2019 ad campaign that shows bicycle delivery riders crashing into invisible walls on the road, and cars with timers marking lines on the road to show the five-minute barrier that cannot be crossed.

This is a great example of Withholding. No hot subs. No delivery beyond a certain point. As Will Burns explains in a 2019 *Forbes* article, "sometimes saying no is the best way to get customers to say yes."

Jimmy John's took flaunting to the next level with their Home in the Zone contest. Customers who had homes outside of the five-minute delivery zone could apply to win a brand-new house, which was located close enough to be eligible for freaky fast delivery.

Jimmy John's doesn't apologize for not delivering to homes or businesses outside of the restricted radius. They aren't going to change. But you could. Just move. Buy a new house inside the zone. Get a new job at a company inside the zone. It's not their fault. It's your fault. You're too far away. Get closer.

Has Withholding hurt Jimmy John's? Nope. The franchise was named #1 on the *Entrepreneur* Franchise 500 and has now grown to over 2,800 locations. They are also #2 on the list of Most Popular Restaurants for Business Meals. That sounds a lot like Alignment, which we will talk about in the next section. Business people want fast meals. Jimmy John's delivers. Literally.

Sometimes a Pink Goldfish won't bring hot sandwiches to your house.

Buc-ees goes big - On July 28, 1982, Arch Aplin III opened his first convenience store in Texas. Early on, he decided he'd need a good name and a good logo, something he could build on. The logo and name was an ode to his childhood nickname of "Beaver" and his beloved hunting dog named Buck. That convenience store was named Buc-ees. From its earliest days according to their website, the store has "been committed to providing a clean, friendly, and in stock experience for our customers."

Buc-ees stores are notable for many reasons. In 2012, the chain won a nationwide restroom contest sponsored by Cintas. Buc-ees was not afraid to flaunt it, creating a billboard with the following message, "Top Two Reasons to Stop at Buc-ee's: #1 and #2." In 2016 *Bon Appétit* named Buc-ee's "America's Best Rest Stop" in honor of its food. Their New Braunfels, Texas location, at 68,000 square feet, has been recognized as the World's Largest C-store" by the National Association of Convenience Stores.

But the thing that makes Buc-ees stand out amongst any other highway rest stop is their Withholding stance against truck drivers. Sorry, 18-wheelers are not allowed at any Buc-ees.

Sometimes a Pink Goldfish doesn't welcome truckers.

PERSONAL BRANDING PROFILE

David Rendall experiences the pressure to grow on a regular basis. As a speaker, he works on his own with no full-time employees. He has no plans to grow, other than doing more speeches. He doesn't want to offer other services or expand into other businesses.

When people find this out, they regularly tell him that speaking doesn't scale. In other words, you can't grow it into a billion-dollar business like Amazon or Tesla. Additionally, David's business is dependent on his presence to deliver the speech. Businesses that scale can become independent of the founder and can generate income without the founder's ongoing involvement. All of that is true, to some extent, but it misses the point.

David doesn't want to scale his business. David wants to work by himself and for himself. David doesn't want to manage employees. David doesn't want to run a business. David wants to speak. That's what he enjoys. That's what he's good at doing.

Additionally, a small business is a good fit for his other goals. Being a small business allows him time to spend with his family and to train extensively for Ironman triathlons and other endurance races. It's less money and fame but more of what matters to him. As Dan Pink says in *Free Agent Nation*, "Bigger isn't better. Better is better."

PINK PROFILE

It all started with the blackest black, Vantablack, which was created by Surrey Nanosystems. The scientific explanation of how they made something so black and why it looks so black is so confusing that we are going to just skip over that part. Just trust us. It's really, really, really black.

Then Anish Kapoor, a very famous artist, bought the exclusive rights to use Vantablack. No one else can use it without his permission. No one. Ever.

You probably haven't heard of Anish Kapoor, but you would recognize his work. For example, he designed Cloud Gate also known as "The Bean" in Millenium Park in Chicago among many other well-known works of art throughout the world. You've seen it, even if you don't know it. It's coated in reflective chrome and has appeared in TV shows, movies, and millions of Instagram posts.

Continued...

You almost certainly haven't heard of Stuart Semple. He is a relatively unknown artist. He found out about Vantablack from his mom and was outraged that no other artists had access to it. So he fought back by creating the Pinkest Pink and selling it on one condition. Anyone can buy it, except for Anish Kapoor. Anyone who purchases it must agree to the following statement.

> By adding this product to your cart you confirm that you are not Anish Kapoor, you are in no way affiliated to Anish Kapoor, you are not purchasing this item on behalf of Anish Kapoor or an associate of Anish Kapoor. To the best of your knowledge, information and belief this paint will not make its way into the hands of Anish Kapoor.

Semple didn't expect to sell a lot of pink, he was just trying to make a point. But the demand for pinkest pink was huge and he was nearly overwhelmed as he tried to fulfill the avalanche of orders. He ended up enlisting family members to help.

Of course, Anish Kapoor eventually got his hands on the pinkest pink. He dipped his middle finger in it and posted a photo on *Instagram*.

Photo Credit: *Instagram*

But Semple had made his point and had galvanized the art community against Kapoor and his Vantablack hoarding. He had also become much more well-known than when he started.

Continued...

He used his new popularity to engage other artists in an effort to create an affordable and accessible black that would be nearly as good as Vantablack. He created Black 1.0, sent hundreds of samples out, and asked people to try to make it blacker. They did and the result is Black 2.0.

We love this story because it's about pink and black, but also because it's about Withholding. Anish Kapoor withheld Vantablack from everyone, and Stuart Semple withheld the Pinkest Pink from Anish Kapoor, and, in the process, they brought an obscure scientific breakthrough to the attention of people who would otherwise never have known about it. Kapoor became even more famous and Semple went from unknown to famous and admired, at least in the world of artists. There is power in Withholding.

Sometimes a Pink Goldfish is the Pinkest Pink Goldfish ever and Anish Kapoor can't have it.

The W in F.L.A.W.S.O.M.E. is for Withholding, doing less. Let's move on to the S...

CHAPTER 10

SWERVING

"Without deviation progress is not possible."

— Frank Zappa

THE S IN F.L.A.W.S.O.M.E. STANDS FOR SWERVING

Swerving is about deviating, diverging, and veering. The emphasis here is on relatively small differentiation efforts. After reading about Flaunting, Lopsiding, Avoiding, and Withholding, it's easy to feel like differentiation requires massive changes to your brand or strategy. That's not always true. Sometimes you just need to turn a little bit to get away from the herd.

It's very common for brands to homogenize. As we look at what successful companies are doing, it's natural to emulate them. This has even been institutionalized in the process of benchmarking. We try to find out what others are doing right and then do the same thing. It sounds reasonable, but there's a problem.

When everyone in an industry starts copying the leaders, then, over time, the entire industry starts to look the same, feel the same, and sound the same. There are no differences. Nothing distinguishes one brand from another. It's herds of cows and zebras, and everyone's competing to be even more like the competition.

As Youngme Moon explains in *Different - Escaping the Competitive Herd*, "The dynamic is not unlike a popularity contest in which everyone tries to win by being equal parts friendly, happy, active, and fun. Or an election campaign in which all the candidates try to be charming, serious, humble, and strong. Once everyone starts doing it, no one stands out." It's a downward spiral of conformity, a veritable sea of crushing sameness.

If you want to stop the spiral, you don't have to run away at full speed. You can simply take a step in a different direction. It doesn't have to be the opposite direction—we'll get to that in the next chapter—just a different direction. You don't have to turn completely around, just a little to the right or a little to the left, and then keep going. It's okay to go slowly—just make sure to start going, start Swerving.

One last note. Swerving is a good place to start before committing everything to a massive overhaul of your organization. Experiment. Do a pilot. Start small.

Swerving occupies the middle of both the STRUT and SUBTRACT quadrants.

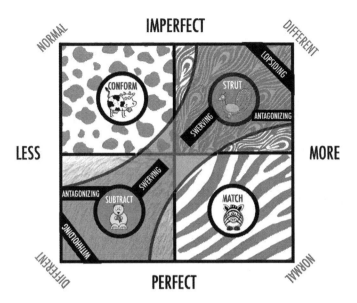

Swerving involves doing a little MORE of what makes you different and doing a little LESS of what is considered normal by others.

Want a strong example of Swerving? Let's head outside.

Since 2015, REI has closed its stores and its website on Black Friday. They call it #OptOutside. It was a purposeful move to separate itself from other retailers. Instead of hitting the mall, the company wants customers to hit the trail. They are encouraging their employees and customers to go for a hike.

"We really want this to be a day when people are outdoors, spending time with their families," says Jerry Stritzke, REI's former CEO. Taking care of employees has always been important. REI has been ranked in the top 100 Companies to Work For in the United States by *Fortune* since 1985, which earned it a place in the *Fortune* Hall of Fame.

According to reporting by the *Washington Post*, industry analysts say they're seeing a [Black Friday] backlash as consumers realize they can often get the same discounts days or weeks later without having to rush out on a holiday.[25] "Black Friday has lost its significance," says Steven J. Barr, consumer markets leader for PwC. "Retailers have conditioned the consumer to believe everything's on sale every day, which means the deals on Black Friday are not significantly different from any other time."

---

25. https://www.washingtonpost.com/news/business/wp/2017/10/30/rei-thinks-you-have-better-things-to-do-than-shop-on-black-friday/

Roughly 35 percent of consumers who planned to shop during Thanksgiving week in 2017 said they would do so on Black Friday, down from 51 percent in 2016 and 59 percent the year before, according to consumer markets research from PwC. "Black Friday has gotten weaker and weaker," said Stritzke. "It's becoming less important."

In 2015, when REI announced it would remain closed on Black Friday, it was regarded as a radical move in an industry that relies heavily on holiday shopping. And messing with Black Friday, which is historically the most lucrative day of the year for many retailers, seemed risky. But the swerve paid dividends. In 2017, REI expanded the #OptOutside campaign by creating an online search engine for people to find nearby opportunities for activities such as hiking, rowing, and rock climbing.

How has this deviation from traditional retailers affected their business? Sales, profits, and revenues keep increasing every year. Being closed on the biggest shopping day hasn't hurt them. Instead, it has helped them and maybe made the world a better place.

REI's radical approach to Black Friday is working but it isn't really spreading. In 2018, only one other retailer was closed on Black Friday when Title Nine, a women's sportswear company, debuted their #girlsdayout. However, they didn't follow REI in closing their website. It can be hard to go against standard industry practices. It can be hard to swerve, but it works.

Sometimes a Pink Goldfish is an empty store on Black Friday.

The Carolina Hurricanes are a "Bunch of Jerks" - It all started in 2019 when Don Cherry ripped the Carolina Hurricanes hockey team for their creative post-game celebrations.[26] The 85-year-old Canadian hockey TV commentator, known for wearing attention-seeking suits, called the team a "bunch of jerks" for their antics. From that point, the Hurricanes quickly took on the moniker as something of a badge of honor.

By the next day, they started promoting shirts with "Bunch of Jerks" written on the front and their team logo beneath it. This was a great swerve. It's short-term. It won't be relevant for too long, but they were unapologetic, instead of ashamed.

Sometimes a Pink Goldfish is a jerk.

Beale's leverages a complaint - YOUR MANAGER IS BITCH. This is a new beer from Beale's Brewery. Notice the lack of an "A"? It is intentional. The beer was inspired by a customer who was refused service. Here's the email they sent:

---

26. https://wjla.com/sports/washington-capitals/why-carolina-hurricanes-calling-themselves-bunch-of-jerks

Subject: Y'all suck
Message: Your manager is bitch and your beer tastes like old hot OJ.

What would you do with this customer complaint? Apologize? Delete? Or would you take the Pink Goldfish route of Antagonizing?

Beale's used it to call out inappropriate behavior and salute everyone in the service industry. They put the picture of their GM on the can and lauded her when launching it. They describe the beer on *UNTAPPD*, "Meet BC. She started with us as a server when Beale's opened, worked her way up to bartender and now GM. She's kept our team together throughout the past year, gracefully navigating every new challenge thrown her way."

The back of the can shares a picture of the email complaint with a note:[27]

> This beer is a love letter to all of the service industry workers who, despite a global pandemic, endeavor each day to provide a safe, welcoming environment for their guests. While we can't prevent verbal abuse... we will continue to call it out and stand with you.

Brandon Wenard at *BroBible* puts it right, "Bravo to Beale's Beer for this one, doing the right thing by supporting their GM who reacted appropriately with a bad customer. Something tells me that when this complainer ends up "taking their business elsewhere," it won't hurt their revenue. Sounds like it's already a hit and they'll be brewing more YOUR MANAGER IS BITCH in no-time."[28]

Sometimes a Pink Goldfish is a beer with bad grammar.

Progressive knows that people hate Flo – Progressive is one of the largest insurance companies in the United States. The company was started in Ohio in 1937 by Jack Green and Joseph Lewis. One of their initial differentiation strategies was focusing on insurance for risky drivers. Then, in 2008, they added Flo.

Flo is the extremely enthusiastic and upbeat fictional customer service representative in the bright white uniform with the nametag. Some people love her. They think she is funny and cute and quirky and energetic and memorable. Others find her incredibly annoying. She's been compared to the AFLAC duck with the grating voice of Gilbert Gottfried. Haters describe her as "irritating, creepy, dorky, unattractive, and weird."

27   https://untappd.com/b/beale-s-your-manager-is-bitch/4131833/photos
28.   https://brobible.com/culture/article/virginia-beales-beer-manager-email/

Flo's commercials appear on lists of the most disliked advertisements, and there are "I Hate Flo" groups on *Facebook*, including one calling for "No Mo Flo."[29]

Flo is polarizing. Many people dislike her, but everyone knows who she is. And that's the point. She has helped Progressive get, and keep, the attention of potential customers.

Sometimes a Pink Goldfish wears a while apron.

Voodoo Doughnut prescribes medicine – Kenneth "Cat Daddy" Pogson and Tres Shannon founded Voodoo Doughnut in Portland, Oregon, in 2003. They chose "voodoo" because they liked the number of O's in the word. This is obviously a very scientific approach to the branding process.

To set themselves apart from the standard doughnut shops of the world, the pair decided to create toppings in an entirely new way. Their maple doughnut is layered with two full strips of bacon. Other doughnuts are covered in Cap'n Crunch or Fruit Loops cereal. "We reinvented the doughnut shop," says Tres. "Everyone can say what they want, but no one was putting strips of bacon on a maple doughnut before us. No one was using cereal!"

Their signature doughnut is an edible voodoo doll. It's a plain doughnut with a face and arms and is covered with chocolate frosting and white decorations. A pretzel stick is included and can be used to stab the doll, which is filled with red jelly.

During shop hours, the pair experimented with new ingredients that began to turn heads. "The Nyquil doughnut really built up the hype around us," says Cat Daddy. "All of a sudden, we were on wacky morning radio talk shows all around the country. They talked about us on *The Wire*, Jay Leno mentioned us; it was madness especially for our first few months in business."

A doughnut covered in Pepto Bismol and crushed Tums was next. But both of the drug-laced doughnuts have been removed from the menu. The Portland Health Department determined that it wasn't safe for people to consume either one of these pharmaceutical pastries. Having your doughnut banned by a government agency definitely counts as a step toward antagonizing.

If that wasn't enough, their Cock'N'Balls doughnut definitely antagonizes some visitors to their stores. We won't describe it for you here, but you can find a complete description on their website.

Voodoo Doughnut is also unusual in two other small ways. They only accept cash payments, and their signature pink boxes are famous worldwide. Additionally, you can see the "Keep Portland

---

Weird" sign from the front of Voodoo Doughnut. They are definitely doing their part to fulfill that goal. We'll discuss weird places more in the final chapter.

Sometimes a Pink Goldfish is a Nyquil doughnut that is banned by the government.

Nurse Next Door embraces happier aging – Established in Vancouver in 2001, Nurse Next Door provides home healthcare services for senior citizens. With competition in the home healthcare space intensifying, Nurse Next Door needed to stand out from its competitors with a brand refresh that portrays both the company and its clients as vibrant, fun-loving, and caring.

In 2017, the brand launched the Happier Aging campaign. Even though future clients were part of the Woodstock Generation, Arif Abdulla, VP of Global Franchise Development, says the industry still tends to present seniors in the wrong light. "We're an industry that's highly competitive, but also highly stale," he said. "If you look at our industry, it's filled with clinical, stale, muted imagery that doesn't really portray seniors in the way they see themselves." To combat this, the brand hired a full-time photographer/videographer for its team.

The brand believes that aging is something to be celebrated. "Happier Aging" means reconnecting seniors with interests, hobbies, and passions that might have gotten lost amid busy schedules, health concerns, or other distractions.

One of the videos in the Happier Again campaign is a video of a Nurse Next Door Care Designer named Stephanie. She talks about working with Miss Daisy, a wheelchair-bound senior in her mid 80s, to write her bucket list. The first item describes how Miss Daisy missed gardening. Stephanie helped her establish a tabletop garden.

The second item on her list was a bit more risqué. Miss Daisy wanted to see a male stripper. Stephanie says on the video, "Why not! Happier Aging is about living your life and having no boundaries." After receiving permission from her son, the caregiver brought Miss Daisy to the show *Thunder Down Under*. Miss Daisy had a wonderful time.

Is Happier Aging leading to a happier bottom-line? As of 2019, the franchise had experienced a 5-year growth rate of 151 percent. Nurse Next Door has also garnered numerous business awards including placing top 50 on *Entrepreneur's* Franchise 500 list and being named the fifth best mid-sized franchise system in North America by *Franchise Business Review*.

Sometimes a Pink Goldfish is a strong man in a thong.

HVLS is unapologetically big - Research shows that if you keep cows cooler, they eat more and produce more milk. Carey Smith learned this while employed at a company that produced large fans for barns. He foresaw industrial applications and founded a small manufacturing company in Lexington, Kentucky in 1999.

He called it the HVLS Fan Company. Their first commercial fan spanned 20 feet. HVLS was an acronym for High Velocity Low Speed. Descriptive? Yes. Boring? Absolutely.

But once HVLS started embracing its uniqueness, the company began its transformation into an international industry leader. Smith shared with *Inc.*, "When we answered the phone 'HLVS Fan Co.,' the people on the other end of the line would pause for a few seconds because those letters meant nothing to them. Then they'd ask, 'Are you the guys who make those big-ass fans?'"

It began with a donkey in their marketing. That photo shoot started the ball rolling. Soon after they leaned in and swerved by renaming the company, BIG ASS FANS.

Not everyone appreciated it. Swerving will create resistance.

A postmaster refused to deliver their first run of postcards. A councilman wanted a billboard removed from their manufacturing facility. The Lexington Bluegrass Airport rejected their request to advertise and their offer to provide FREE fans.

The company took the heat, stayed cool, and stuck with the weird name. Carey Smith shared with *Inc.*, "To this day, we receive a small amount of hate mail from people who find the name offensive, crude, or inappropriate. We embrace the haters by posting videos of their rants. Most people just think it's funny and get as much of a kick out of the hate mail as we do."

Carey Smith got the last laugh. He sold the company for $500 million in 2017.

There's one more distinction that we think might be helpful. HVLS swerved and became Big Ass Fans, slowly and organically. They followed the lead of their customers and discovered a way to differentiate their otherwise boring fan company.

However, they've also been willing to swerve back slightly and sporadically. They remove the Big Ass Fans name and logo from fans that are sold to churches, schools, and governments. Offending children and religious people unnecessarily isn't part of their strategy. Similarly, they have some targeted advertisements and videos that simply talk about Big Fans. Sometimes they antagonize, like when they mock the people who send them hate mail. But other times, they respect people and groups with different values and make small and reasonable exceptions. This is one of the best examples of swerving that we've found.

Sometimes high velocity, low speed fans are really just Big Ass Fans.

PERSONAL BRANDING PROFILE

Bert Kreischer is a stand-up comedian. If you've ever seen him perform, you'll remember. He's a straight, white, and middle-aged man. That's not very unique. So how does he differentiate himself? He swerves and does his shows shirtless. To be clear, he is not fit. You will not see washboard abs. He doesn't seem to be a fan of manscaping either. He's hairy and overweight and proud of it. He shows it off by taking it off. His willingness to expose his imperfect body makes him stand out in the world of stand up.

Sometimes a Pink Goldfish is a bare-chested comic.

PINK PROFILE

It was 1893 in London, and Douglas Macrae, publisher of the *Financial Times*, was looking for a way to distinguish his newspaper from the competition, the *Financial and Mining News*. He decided to start using pink paper in order to stand out, explaining it this way:

> In order to provide outward features which will distinguish the *Financial Times* from other journals, a new heading and distinctive features will be introduced, and the paper will be slightly tinted.

An article in *Braithwaite* argues that the decision to use pink paper "would turn out to be the most significant branding step the company would ever take."

Initially, it was cheaper to use pink paper than to print on white paper. This is because paper has to be bleached in order to make it white. It is somewhat pink earlier in the process, so they didn't need to dye the paper to make it pink. They just eliminated a step in the process.

However, pink became such a powerful part of their brand that they made the paper even pinker over the years, and now they actually pay extra to keep the color just right. They even extended the pink onto the background of their current website.

It is important to note that this wasn't a big decision at the time. Even the paper described the new color as "slightly tinted." This was a small change, a swerve. It wasn't a huge transformation. It was a swerve. But it was a minor adjustment that had a major impact.

Continued...

More than 125 years have passed since the *Financial Times* went pink and they are still going strong. As other newspapers are disappearing in response to the rise of digital and social media, they are thriving. In a 2015 article in *Quartz*, Zachary Seward described them as "one of the world's most distinctive news brands." Indeed, they were sold to Nikkei that same year for $1.3 billion. Sometimes, little pink changes make a big difference.

The S in F.L.A.W.S.O.M.E. is for Swerving, small deviations. Let's move on to the O...

CHAPTER 11

OPPOSING

"Be fearful when others are greedy,
and be greedy when others are fearful."

— Warren Buffett

THE "O" IN F.L.A.W.S.O.M. STANDS FOR OPPOSING

Opposing is doing the exact opposite of what others are doing. It's being *unlike* the competition. It's doing things that conflict with traditional methods.

Opposing sits in the top left of the STRUT quadrant in the matrix.

Opposing brands are unlike other brands. They are contradictory and dissimilar. They operate in a way that is incompatible with everyone else. Opposing involves defying, resisting, and fighting. It's refusing to give in, to yield, to submit, to surrender to the pressure to conform, to fit in, to follow the crowd.

Opposing is simple. When everyone goes left, you go right. When everyone offers healthy options, you offer unhealthy ones. When everyone is open late, you close early.

This isn't like Swerving. It isn't a slight deviation from the norm. It's maximum separation. It's a complete break with convention.

It's worth taking a brief look at the definition of opposite.[30] It means, "contrary or radically different in some respect common to both, as in nature, qualities, direction, result, or significance."

---

30. http://www.dictionary.com/browse/opposite

This is interesting. To be opposites, two things need to be both very different and also have something in common. There's something that unites them but something else that completely separates them.

For example, being a tall person is the opposite of being a short person. Both are people, but they are opposites as it relates to height. However, being a tall person isn't the opposite of being a fat person. They are both people, but height and weight are just different qualities, not opposites. Fat and skinny are opposites. There has to be a similar method of comparing things for them to be opposites, and they also have to maintain some similarities.

So what? Why does this matter? It's important, because everything doesn't have to be different in order to be the opposite. In fact, if everything is different when you compare two things, they're not opposites. They are unrelated.

In other words, you don't have to leave your industry to do the opposite of what everyone else in your industry does. That's not doing the opposite. That's just joining or creating a different industry. Paradoxically, you have to maintain some similarities in order to be considered opposites.

For example, they sell socks in stores. You sell them online. They charge for shipping. You provide free shipping. They sell socks in packs of six pairs. You sell them one pair at a time. They sell long socks. You sell short socks. These are all examples of doing the opposite.

If you start selling hats instead of socks, this isn't the opposite. It's just different. Although it is the opposite in the sense that you are covering heads while they are covering feet, opposite ends of the body.

Opposing occupies the top of the flaunting zone, just to the right of the centerline. Brands here are fully embracing what makes them weird or imperfect. When everyone goes in one direction with the herd, opposing brands do the exact opposite.

Elon Musk's three companies, Tesla, Solar City, and SpaceX are quintessential examples of Opposing, starting with the fact that he runs three companies. This is the opposite of most entrepreneurs who focus on a single company or idea, or at least just one at a time.

Let's start with Tesla, the disruptive electric car company. Tesla vehicles use electricity, instead of gasoline. Their cars can be updated constantly via software updates, instead of yearly through the release of a new model. They are also pioneering self-driving car technology, instead of promoting the human-driving experience.

Instead of offering financing, like a traditional car company, Tesla actually collects a pre-payment before even producing the vehicle. This is not a small difference. In 2016, Tesla announced the

Model 3 and received 325,000 reservations, at a cost of $1,000 each, in the first week. This provided them with $325 million in capital to begin production and make other crucial investments more than a year before ever delivering a single vehicle.

Solar City, a solar-power company founded by Elon Musk and his brother, Kimbal, has the goal of offering free battery recharging to Tesla owners. This is in obvious opposition to the high fuel prices being paid by traditional car owners.

SpaceX is Musk's space exploration company, founded with the goal of building a human colony on Mars. Previously, it was only large countries that could build and maintain a space program. It was widely believed that it was simply too expensive and unprofitable for a company to take on. Musk proved that a private organization could do what it seemed like only public organizations could do.

One of the ways he accomplished this was with another Opposing move. The cost of disposable rockets was one of the primary barriers to efficient space travel. By pioneering reusable rockets, SpaceX has dramatically reduced the expenses related to leaving Earth.

Sometimes creating a Pink Goldfish is not brain surgery, just rocket science.

Let's take a closer look at Opposing with some additional examples.

Little Missmatched doesn't sell matching pairs of socks – Little Missmatched sells socks that don't match, and they do it on purpose. The company was founded in 2004 with the goal of "disrupting the marketplace by reinventing a category." Their values include individuality and empowerment for girls.

Normal socks are sold in pairs. Each sock in the pair matches the other one. That's how socks work. Every year, people spend millions of hours on laundry trying to match their socks. Every year, millions of socks are lost, leaving a single sock with no matching partner.

But what if socks didn't need to match? David's friend Kenan wears mismatched socks. Kenan explained that he doesn't like to waste time matching socks. When he folds clothes, he just combines the first two socks he finds into a pair.

Little Missmatched opposes the norm by selling socks in sets of three, none of which match each other. They also encourage girls to be unique by wearing distinctive socks that don't conform to traditional ideas of how they should dress. They tell girls they have the right to "not be like everyone else" and to show off their "kooky personality." They show girls that it can be fun to do the opposite of what everyone else is doing.

Sometimes a Pink Goldfish is three socks that don't match.

The Barkley Marathons don't want you to finish – In 1977, James Earl Ray, convicted of assassinating Martin Luther King Jr., escaped from Brushy Mountain State Penitentiary in the mountains of Tennessee. After 55 hours, he was found just eight miles away from the prison. Gary "Lazarus Lake" Cantrell thought he could have gone at least 100 miles in the time it took Ray to go just eight. He couldn't, but this gave him an idea for a race, named after his friend Barry Barkley, in the same rugged environment. The Barkley Marathons were born.

It turns out that professional athletes can't run 100 miles over the brutal terrain either. Only 15 runners have completed the course since the race was started in 1986. In 2006, 30 of the 40 participants were unable to even complete the first two miles.

Let's look at how the Barkley Marathons are the opposite of normal races.

Normal marathons have a clear online registration process. The Barkley Marathons have no clear registration process. If you want to race, you need to mail a letter to the race organizer and hope he responds.

Normal marathons use timing chips to track runners on the course and as they finish. The Barkley Marathons have no electronic timing. Runners collect pages from paperback books at various milestones along the way to prove they've completed the course. For example, if you are runner #22, you rip out page #22 from the book at each checkpoint and bring it back with you to the finish line in a plastic bag.

Normal marathons provide course markers and maps as well as volunteers to clearly guide runners. The Barkley Marathons do not have a marked course. There is only one map. The course changes each year. You can't take the official map with you, but you can make one for yourself. Each time you finish a lap—there are five 20-mile laps—you have to do the next lap in the opposite direction, just to make navigation that much more difficult.

Normal marathons offer aid stations with drinks, snacks, water, ice, and medical care. The Barkley Marathons have no aid stations or volunteers or any assistance of any kind. Runners are on their own. They have to provide all supplies and carry everything with them.

Normal marathons charge a fee of around $100 to cover expenses or to donate to charity. The Barkley Marathons charge an application fee of $1.60. Participants also have to bring Lazarus, the race organizer, a license plate from their state/country and an additional fee that changes from year to year. One year the fee was a pack of tube socks. Another year it was a button-down shirt in the race organizer's size.

Normal marathons provide a clear start time for the race. The Barkley Marathons have no set start time. A race starts an hour after the race organizer blows the conch shell. It officially starts when he lights his cigarette.

Normal marathons have major corporate sponsors and advertising throughout the course. The Barkley Marathons have no sponsors and no advertising.

The Barkley Marathon is so unusual and so interesting that it was the subject of a very popular *Netflix* documentary with the subtitle, "The Race That Eats Its Young." It is one of the most desirable races for endurance runners throughout the world.

Sometimes a Pink Goldfish is a race that you can't sign up for and can't finish.

The Barkley Marathons are incredibly hard and the Boerne .5k is incredibly easy - Reading about the Barkley Marathons might leave you feeling like the only way to create a successful race is to make it ridiculously difficult. So you're trying to figure out some diabolical plan for the world's most brutal challenge. But that's getting trapped in the benchmarking mindset of following the leaders and trying to mimic the success stories. Remember, you can always do the opposite.

If you want to raise money for a great nonprofit cause, you don't have to create a Barkley Marathon competitor, but you should probably avoid the traditional 5k race. There are so many of those, you'll struggle to get anyone's attention, which means that you won't get a lot of participants and you won't raise very much money.

Here's what they did in Boerne, Texas, a small town with a population of less than 20,000 people, about 30 miles outside of San Antonio. They wanted to raise money for Blessings in a Backpack, a nonprofit that provides a backpack full of food for kids to take home from school to get them through the weekend.

Instead of the ubiquitous five-kilometer race, they invited people to participate in a .5k run. America is not on the metric system, so we'll translate. Half a kilometer is .31 miles or 546 yards or 1,638 feet. Even at a slow walking pace, you could finish the distance in less than eight minutes. Some have called it "America's Laziest Race." Others claim it is "The World's Shortest Road Race."

One of their goals is to be a safe haven for all the underachievers who don't want to wake up early on the weekend to workout or finish a race. And you don't have to wake up early for the Boerne .5k. It starts at 11am. They know their audience. You can sleep in and still get to the race on time.

When you arrive at the race, you'll receive a pre-race beer. Don't worry, if you finish your beer in the few minutes that you're doing the race, they also provide a post-race beer.

But what about your needs during the race? What if you get tired or thirsty or hungry along the way? Are there aid stations on the course? Yes. There is an aid station at the halfway point, where you can get coffee and donuts. It also includes a smoking section, just in case it's been too long since your last cigarette and you can't wait another four minutes until the end of the race.

When you cross the finish line, just moments after you crossed the start line, you'll get a finisher medal, race T-shirt, and a .5k race sticker for your car, so you can let all the other drivers know about your athletic prowess.

But maybe you don't have what it takes to go the full distance. Maybe you haven't trained enough. Maybe you didn't sleep well. Maybe you just don't like to move at all. That's okay. You can be a VIP. Pay double the entry fee and you can get a ride in a vintage Volkswagen bus to the finish line. No running or walking required. VIPs still get a medal, shirt, and sticker, even though they didn't exert any energy.

This is ridiculous. This is outrageous. So does it work? It does.

The race is so popular that they sold out all 225 spots in their first year and raised over $20,000 for charity. The 2019 race sold out in only 37 minutes. This just led to even more creativity.

They created a virtual option, which allows participants to sit at home and watch someone else complete the course with a GoPro camera mounted on their head. This allows for unlimited participants from anywhere in the world, which maximizes the donations they can receive. In fact, they've had more virtual registrations, 1,500, than regular registrations. Virtual participants even get a shirt, medal, and race sticker, even though they haven't gotten off their couch. No discrimination. No judgment.

Their race has been featured in national publications like *Men's Journal* and *The Washington Post*. How many local races get that kind of attention?

Is it sustainable or is it just a gimmick? The 2020 race had an increased capacity of 1,000 and sold out in hours.

Sometimes a Pink Goldfish is a race you can't lose.

Are you willing to murder your thirst and put an end to bottled water? If so, Liquid Death Mountain Water could be your willing accomplice.

Liquid Death is a strong example of Opposing. They operate in a way that is incompatible with everyone else in the category. Opposing is refusing to surrender to the pressure to fit in or follow the crowd.

The brand is clear in its deliberate approach to differentiation. In their words, "Let's be clear. Liquid Death is a completely unnecessary approach to bottled water. In fact, we strive to be unnecessary in everything we do. Because unnecessary things tend to be far more interesting, fun, hilarious, captivating, memorable, exciting, and cult-worthy than 'necessary' things."

Their goal is to take the world's healthiest beverage and make it just as unnecessarily entertaining as the unhealthy drink and snack brands. They challenge, "Why should unhealthy products be the only brands with 'permission' to be loud, fun, and weird?"

For some, being bad never felt so good. Liquid Death canned water shines a light on the wasteful impact of plastic bottles.

Patagonia doesn't want you to buy their clothes – Most clothing retailers want you to buy their clothes. In fact, they spend a tremendous amount of time and money trying to convince you to visit their stores and buy their stuff. That's why it was surprising in 2011 when Patagonia placed an ad in *The New York Times* telling people not to buy one of their jackets. To be clear, Patagonia paid money on Black Friday for an opportunity to push people away from their stores on the biggest shopping day of the year.

Patagonia is so serious about sustainability and environmental responsibility that they want customers to think twice before buying new clothes. The company explained their reasoning this way:

> It's part of our mission to inspire and implement solutions to the environmental crisis. It would be hypocritical for us to work for environmental change without encouraging customers to think before they buy. To reduce environmental damage, we all have to reduce consumption as well as make products in more environmentally sensitive, less harmful ways.... It's folly to assume that a healthy economy can be based on buying and selling more and more things people don't need—and it's time for people who believe that's folly to say so.

Their goal is to create products that last longer and are replaced less often. In this way, they can stay in business and stay true to their values. But they need cooperation from consumers in order to make their vision a reality.

Worn Wear is another way that Patagonia is doing the opposite of most clothing retailers. They buy back used Patagonia clothing, clean it, repair it, and then resell it. The company explains:[31]

> Worn Wear is a set of tools to help our customers partner with Patagonia to take mutual responsibility to extend the life of the products Patagonia makes and customers purchase. The program provides significant resources for responsible care, repair, reuse and resale, and recycling at the end of a garment's life.

Does this Opposing approach work? Yes. Patagonia has revenues of more than $800 million and they recently won the UN's Champions of the Earth Award. Additionally, Yvon Chouinard's net worth is $1.2 billion and most of that is based on the value of his company.

Sometimes a Pink Goldfish is a used jacket.

Burger King recommends their biggest competitor - In 2020, Burger King UK stood up for its employees and the industry by taking an Opposing strategy. Instead of pushing their own products, the restaurant began recommending McDonald's during the COVID-19 global pandemic. "We know, we never thought we'd be saying this either," said the brand on *Facebook*.

Here is the full message:

> ORDER FROM McDONALD'S.
>
> We never thought we'd be asking you to do this. Just like we never thought we'd be encouraging you to order from KFC, Subway, Domino's Pizza, Pizza Hut, Five Guys, Greggs, Taco Bell, Papa John's, Leon ... or any of the other independent food outlets, too numerous to mention here. In short, any of our sister food chains (fast or not so fast).
>
> We never thought we'd be asking you to do this, but restaurants employing thousands of staff really need your support at the moment.
>
> So, if you want to help, keep treating yourself to tasty meals through home delivery, takeaway or drive-thru. Getting a whopper is always best, but ordering a Big Mac is also not such a bad thing.
>
> Take care,
> Team Burger King UK

---

31. https://hypebeast.com/2017/9/patagonia-worn-wear-launch

This is a bold whopper of an Opposing move. A month later, Burger King launched an *Instagram* campaign where they went one step further. They began advertising the competition on their page.

Sometimes a Pink Goldfish promotes other goldfish.

Kazakhstan stops fighting and starts flaunting - "VERY NICE!" If you are not familiar with the phrase, it's commonly used by Borat, the Kazakh movie character created by Sasha Baron Cohen. And it is now being used by Kazakhstan in a new tourism campaign. The ads feature tourists hiking, drinking alcoholic horse milk, meeting locals, and marveling at Kazakh architecture. The country is leaning into the publicity coming from the 2020 sequel entitled *Borat Subsequent Moviefilm*.

This is in stark contrast to how the country railed against the film when the original *Borat* hit theaters. In fact, Kazakhstan is Opposing its own response to the first movie. According to *The Guardian*,

> After its release in 2006, the Kazakh government placed ads in US newspapers disputing some of the film's claims and presenting the country as modern, stable, and outward-looking. The advertisements were timed with a visit from President Nursultan Nazarbayev and featured a photograph of Nazarbayev shaking hands with US President George W. Bush.

The first time, Kazakhstan refused to flaunt their uniqueness and weakness. They tried to fight back and create a more normal image. This time around, they are embracing the Very Nice slogan from the movie. Kairat Sadvakassov, the deputy chairman of Kazakh Tourism shared with the *Huffington Post*, "Kazakhstan's nature is very nice; its food is very nice; and its people, despite Borat's jokes to the contrary, are some of the nicest in the world. We would like everyone to come experience Kazakhstan for themselves by visiting our country."

Sometimes a Pink Goldfish is Very Nice.

Man Crates won't open up - Imagine a gift that comes with a crowbar. Jeremy Watkin of NumberBarn shared his experience with the online gifting company *Man Crates*,

> I received a box that contained a wooden crate similar to the Dad on *A Christmas Story* when he received his "Major Award" that turned out to be a leg lamp. The box also included a crowbar and instructions to "limber up" because these crates are "a stubborn adversary."

Jeremy didn't get a leg lamp. He received a whole set up for making stone-grilled pizzas and was thrilled with the experience. "While I don't consider myself to be a manly man, I felt compelled in that moment to toughen up and accept the challenge of figuring out how to open the crate. I also smiled the entire time and was thrilled when I finally saw the contents."

Man Crates is an Opposing brand when it comes to effort. Shouldn't unboxing be easy? The brand intentionally creates a high-effort experience. Their mission is "to make awesome gifts that guys actually want, gifts that reek of excitement and bring people together. We're in the business of making memories with a hint of mischief."

Jeremy sums up the benefits of this approach, "Unique and fun experiences make for repeat customers and compel them to share with their networks."

Sometimes a Pink Goldfish requires a crowbar.

PERSONAL BRANDING PROFILE

Warren Buffett is one of the richest and most generous people in the world. He explained his formula for success in a *New York Times* article written during the spectacular meltdown of the financial sector in 2008. Buffett's mantra is to do the opposite of what everyone else is doing. "Be fearful when others are greedy. Be greedy when others are fearful." When everyone else zigs, he zags. Avoiding the crowd is what Opposing is all about.

Michael Lewis wrote *The Big Short* to tell the story of the few people who predicted and prepared for the crash of the subprime mortgage industry. One of the people he profiled was Mike Burry, a neurologist in California who has Asperger's syndrome, a form of autism. Burry's investment company, Scion Capital, had returns of 490 percent from 2000 to 2008, when the Standard and Poor's 500 returned only two percent during that same period.

Burry saw the demise of the real estate sector as early as 2005 and made nearly a billion dollars when it imploded. When asked to explain his special insight and willingness to go against the grain, he credited his success to the example of Warren Buffett. Burry believes that "to succeed in a spectacular fashion you have to be spectacularly unusual." We miss out on spectacular success when we are unwilling to be spectacularly unusual.

PINK PROFILE

According to Barbara Nemitz, the author of *Pink: The Exposed Color in Contemporary Culture*, pink contains

> an extraordinary number of contradictory qualities... The pink spectrum can embody practically anything; surface and interior, happiness and suffering, delight and injury, the naive and the corrupt, the sublime and the ordinary, the playful and the existential.

In other words, pink is full of opposites. Pink is also a color that can be used to oppose the competition.

T-Mobile is so committed to pink that they've trademarked their particular version of the color (RAL 4010). They call it magenta, and they aren't messing around. When Aio Wireless started using a similar color (Pantone 676C) in 2014, T-Mobile sued. They argued that "letting Aio continue to use a variant of magenta would cause [T-Mobile] irreparable harm." T-Mobile won the exclusive right to their shade of pink and apparently "nearby colors" as well.

Their CEO, John Legere*, can nearly always be found wearing a pink T-shirt or a satin pink jacket or pink shoes. That's unusual. Most big company CEOs wear suits, not T-shirts. Legere argues that pink and his casual style are part of the company's identity as the "uncarrier," the opposite of the other carriers.

Pink marks T-Mobile as unique from all the other mobile giants who have chosen traditional CEOs and traditional colors, such as blue (AT&T), red (Verizon), yellow (Sprint), and blue/red (US Cellular). Pink isn't a primary color. Experts and studies indicate that most people don't like pink. Using pink as a mass-market corporation is a great example of Opposing. It works because it is an obvious contrast to what the rest of the industry is doing.

* Since writing the first version of Pink Goldfish, John Legere resigned after T-Mobile purchased Sprint to become the third-largest mobile phone carrier in the United States.

The O in F.L.A.W.S.O.M.E. is for Opposing, doing the opposite. Let's move on to the M...

CHAPTER 12

MICRO-WEIRDING

"You have to be odd to be number one."

— Dr. Seuss

THE "M" IN F.L.A.W.S.O.M.E. STANDS FOR MICRO-WEIRDING

Micro-weirding is using minuscule actions to differentiate your brand and customer experience. The lesson is that you can set your brand apart without some cohesive master plan; you can be just a tiny bit weird.

And just because something is micro-weird, doesn't mean it has a micro-impact. The examples in this chapter will show how itty-bitty actions can have a massive impact on your brand.

Micro-weirding occupies the heart of the flaunting zone.

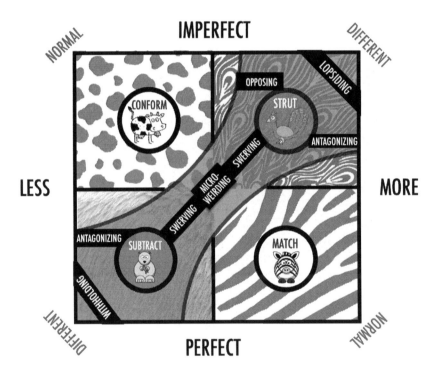

Micro-weirding is doing very small things to stand out. This is the easiest and least risky way to begin creating your Pink Goldfish. If you wanted to organize the ways to flaunt in phases, they would look like this.

- Phase 1: Micro-weirding (low differentiation)
- Phase 2: Swerving & Exposing (moderate differentiation)
- Phase 3: Lopsiding & Withholding (high differentiation)
- Phase 4: Opposing & Antagonizing (massive differentiation)

- In 2009, Stan started searching for companies who purposely put an emphasis on the customer experience by practicing the art of lagniappe. Lagniappe is a creole word that originated in the 1840s in Louisiana. A mix of French and Spanish, it means "the gift" or "to give more." In New Orleans, it was customary for a merchant to do a little something extra at the time of purchase. It was something that was added beyond the transaction to honor the relationship. Any time someone does a little something extra in Louisiana, that's lagniappe.

- Lagniappe is not to be confused with the extra in a baker's dozen. To truly understand a baker's dozen, we need to travel back to its origin in England over 800 years ago. The term dates back to the 13th century during the reign of Henry III. During this time, there was a perceived need for regulations to control quality and check weights to avoid fraudulent activity. The Assize (Statute) of Bread and Ale was instituted to regulate the sale of bread and beer.[32]

Bakers who violated the law could be liable for severe punishment such as losing a hand by the blow of an axe. To guard against the punishment, the baker would give 13 for the price of 12 to be certain of not being known as a cheat. The merchants created the "baker's dozen" concept to change customer perception. They understood that one of the 13 loaves could be lost, eaten, burnt, or ruined in some way and still leave the baker with the original legal dozen. The irony of the Baker's Dozen is that it's not based on the idea of giving a little unexpected extra to the customer to stand out. It was about insurance and covering one's backside for fear of losing a hand.

A CONSCIOUS CHOICE

Micro-weirding is differentiation by experience design. A marketing investment back into your customers so to speak. It's that unexpected surprise that's thrown in for good measure to achieve differentiation, drive retention, and promote word of mouth. After crowdsourcing over 1,001 examples of lagniappe, Stan published *Purple Goldfish* in 2012. This chapter is our way of offering a little something extra to you by sharing examples of companies that do something a little weird.

Here are seven examples:

Popsicles by the pool – When was the last time you had a popsicle? Not recently. When was the last time you had a popsicle at a hotel? You probably haven't. When was the last time you had a popsicle delivered to you at a hotel? Probably never. Have you ever complained because popsicles weren't on the room service menu? Probably not.

So why would a hotel create a popsicle hotline and why would anyone care? In their book, *The Power of Moments*, Chip and Dan Heath categorize the popsicle hotline as a "peak" moment. They

---

32. http://en.wikipedia.org/wiki/Baker%27s_dozen

argue that people value and remember small unusual moments more than larger, seemingly more important ones.

This seems to be true for the Magic Castle Hotel, the highest-rated hotel in the Los Angeles area according to *TripAdvisor*.[33] "Out of over 3,000 reviews on *TripAdvisor*, 94 percent of guests rate the hotel as either 'excellent' or 'very good.'"

But why are the ratings so high? Wouldn't people rather stay at a consistently luxurious property like the Four Seasons? The Magic Castle Hotel doesn't have an amazing pool or beautiful furniture or lovely rooms. It doesn't have most of the things that you'd expect from a great hotel.

What it does have is a Popsicle Hotline. Here's how it works. There's a red phone on a wall by the pool. When you lift the handset, a popsicle specialist answers and takes your order. You don't have to wait long until an employee wearing white gloves brings your popsicles on a silver tray at no charge.

In addition to the Popsicle Hotline, the Magic Castle also has a 24-hour FREE snack bar menu. They offer full sized candy bars, Sour Patch Kids, chips and more in lieu of a minibar.

As the Heath brothers explain, "What the Magic Castle has figured out is that, to delight customers, you need not obsess over every detail. Customers will forgive small swimming pools and underwhelming room décor, as long as you deliver some magical peak moments. The surprise about great service experiences is that they are mostly forgettable." In other words, being micro-weird can be a very valuable differentiation strategy, especially when everyone else is trying to be good at everything.

Sometimes a Pink Goldfish is a red popsicle phone and no minibar.

The new Mercedes-EQS helps you sleep - Mercedes S-Class electric vehicle has a surprising feature that you wouldn't associate with a car. The EQS has a special "Power Nap" program. Just press the button and ...

- the seat reclines
- the windows and the roof sunshade closes
- the interior lighting and temperature adjusts
- the stereo plays relaxing sounds
- the dashboard displays images of a starry night sky

---

33. https://www.tripadvisor.com/Hotel_Review-g32655-d84502-Reviews-Magic_Castle_Hotel-Los_Angeles_California.html

After your nap, the car begins a wake-up routine. No joke, it includes special energizing fragrances and a gentle massage before the seatback rises and the sunshade opens. The scent is called No.6 Mood Linen. It smells like a fig tree surrounded by fresh air.

Sometimes a Pink Goldfish wants you to fall asleep behind the wheel.

It will cost you to be stupid at Tom's Diner - Tom's Diner in Denver, Colorado was founded by Tom Messina in 1999. They became the focus of international attention in January of 2020 when their $.38 charge for stupid questions went viral on social media. Soon after, the story crossed over into traditional media from *The Today Show* in the United States to morning shows in Australia.

This wasn't a random one-time decision by a server or cashier. The cost of a stupid question is listed on the menu next to other side dishes, like coleslaw and fries. It's been there for 20 years.

The current manager said that some people get upset about the charge, but most think it's funny. Many people ask intentionally stupid questions so that they get a receipt with the unusual charge.

Cole slaw	$0.99
French fries	$3.75
Baked potato	$2.99
Cottage cheese	$1.75
Stupid questions	$0.38
Mashed potatoes	$2.99
Vegetarian chili bowl	$4.25

Tom's also offers a couple other unusual items. In the healthy options section, you can opt to "skip your next meal" or "walk home." Both can be added to your bill, but they are free.

Sometimes a Pink Goldfish is a tax on being stupid.

Liberty Tax and its wavers – Accountants are professionals. Taxes are serious business. No one wants to mess with the IRS. That's why it's surprising that Liberty Tax hires wavers to dress up like the Statue of Liberty and sing and dance and wave at the people driving by.

It started accidentally. A Liberty Tax franchise was recording a commercial. During the filming, a costumed actor waved to people and the people waved back. The story made it back to the corporate headquarters, and the marketing department decided to try wavers on a larger scale.

You might think that being a waver is a simple entry-level job and anyone could do it. That is not the case. Potential wavers have to try out for the job. After demonstrating their moves outside, only the best ones are hired.

Wavers dressed up like Lady Liberty are weird, but do they actually impact the business? Liberty's former Chief Marketing Officer, Martha O'Gorman shared they have the data to show that wavers work. She cites increased brand recognition for Liberty—they're competitive with H&R Block—as a sign that taxpayers pay attention to the wavers.

Sometimes a Pink Goldfish is a green statue with a crown.

Dropping the sticky bomb – Joe Sorge opened the Milwaukee restaurant AJ Bombers in 2009, self-described as "Rube Goldberg meets *Willy Wonka and the Chocolate Factory*. Except Rube is into peanuts and Willy Wonka is into crazy Cheeseburgers. And both are very happy about it." One of the micro-weird things is free peanuts for patrons. If you are sitting at a booth, they are shot at you with metal WWII bombers. It doesn't end there. Here are three more signature elements of micro-weirdness from the restaurant:

Oversize beach chairs – a couple of larger than life beach chairs. You feel like a silly little kid while sitting (but isn't that the point).

- Quad cow – take on the quad cow at AJ Bombers. After you've swallowed the last bite of your four-patty burger, you can sign your name on the sacred cow that adorns the wall.
- Sharpies – grab a marker and leave your name or Twitter handle on the wall. You are now part of AJ Bombers.

Sometimes a Pink Goldfish is a metal WWII bomber that delivers peanuts.

Free ice cream or coffee – Stew Leonard grew up the son of a dairy farmer who was in the milk delivery business. The 1960s brought a time of great change for his business. Two things would shake the core of the business. First, the demand for milk delivery was evaporating. Second, the State of Connecticut evoked eminent domain and furrowed the dairy farm to make room for a new highway called Route 7. Pivoting, Stew opened his first dairy store in Norwalk, Connecticut, in 1969. The 17,000 square foot (1,579 square meters) store sold only eight products.

During his first year in business, he was asked by the local elementary school to come out and speak on career day. The principal asked Stew to talk about his store and the dairy business. Even though Stew didn't see the appeal for kids, he reluctantly agreed. As Stew pulled into the parking lot, he knew he was in trouble. There was a fire truck parked in front of the school with kids all around it. It didn't get any better when he walked through the doors of the school. He immediately saw a room with an Air Force officer. A movie about the history of jet airplanes was playing. It was filled with kids. Across the hall was a police officer showing a packed classroom about various police equipment and weapons.

He proceeded to walk down the hall and eventually found his classroom. There was a sign on the door that read "The Dairy Business." Stew entered the room to find only three kids sitting there. Two of who were the sons of his produce manager. For the next 30 minutes he talked about the dairy business and running a store. At the end of the talk, he thanked the kids. Stew then reached into his pocket and handed them each a coupon for a free ice cream. The kids left and Stew waited to present the second of his two Career Day sessions. He waited and waited... no kids. More than

15 minutes passed, still no kids. After 20 minutes the principal came rushing in and exclaimed, "Stew... I don't know what you told those kids, but we have to move your next presentation to the school auditorium." This simple story underscores the impact of word of mouth with the power of a little micro-weirdness.

Today, Stew Leonard's continues the tradition of free ice cream. Customers who purchase $100 or more in groceries get a free ice cream or cup of coffee. It's that little extra or "WOW" according to Stew that makes all the difference.

Sometimes a Pink Goldfish is a free ice cream cone. And speaking of ice cream . . .

Izzy's Ice Cream and mini-scoops – Driven by a desire to run their own business and a genuine love for ice cream, Jeff and Lara Sommers opened the doors to Izzy's Ice Cream in 2000. Together they make more than 150 flavors of ice cream. One of the micro-weird things they do is sampling. For every scoop of ice cream purchased at Izzy's, the buyer gets a little mini-scoop on top for free. The little patented mini-scoop is called the Izzy. It's a little something extra for paying customers.

Sometimes a Pink Goldfish is a mini-scoop of ice cream.

PERSONAL BRANDING PROFILE

Mind the gap. Michael Strahan is a great example of leaning into personal imperfection and micro-weirding. He has a sizable gap between his two front teeth. Strahan shared with *Elle* magazine,[34]

> **ELLE:** You're famous for your gap-toothed smile. Were you ever self-conscious about your looks?

> **STRAHAN:** I was really close to closing it up. I was at the dentist having him do mock-ups. I thought about it, man.

> **ELLE:** That would be like Cindy Crawford removing her mole.

> **STRAHAN:** I was in my twenties. I was playing with the Giants. There's so much pressure to be perfect. You can fix everything now. For me, I made the conscious effort to say "This is who I am." I'm not perfect. I don't want to try to be perfect.

---

34. https://www.elle.com/culture/celebrities/a14357/michael-strahan-interview/

Strahan has now immortalized the gap. Part of being inducted to the Football Hall of Fame involves receiving a bronze bust. While most Hall of Fame statues depict non-smiling players, Strahan insisted his famous gap be included. In an interview with *The New Yorker*,[35] Hall of Fame chief sculptor Blair Buswell discussed Strahan's decision to go smiley:

> Players choose the likeness they prefer (young or old, bearded or clean-shaven), but he (Buswell) typically discourages them from smiling. 'I give them disclosures, and one of them is that bronze teeth never look right,' he said, noting that the former Broncos quarterback John Elway complained, in 2004, that his teeth looked like Chiclets. But Strahan was insistent—I want to be the smiling giant'—so the sculptor agreed. 'I'll do it,' Buswell said. 'I'll just say it's not the most popular choice.'

On March 30, 2021 Strahan announced that he was closing the gap.

Photo Credit: Twitter

Continued...

---

35. https://www.newyorker.com/sports/sporting-scene/blair-buswell-football-artist

It caused an uproar. Then two days later on April 1st, Strahan shared a video via *Twitter* revealing the prank. "Come on, man! The gap is here to stay for a little while. It's not going away any time soon."

Strahan's joke is similar to a ruse pulled by basketball star Anthony Davis in 2018. Davis shared a video in which he apparently shaved his iconic unibrow. It turned out to be a sponsored prank, and The Brow remains strong to this day.

PINK PROFILE

In 2010, Ethan Eyler started a new company called Carstache. They sold big fuzzy mustaches designed to be mounted on the front grill of a car. We'd never heard of them and you probably haven't either.

But the founders of *Lyft*, a ride-sharing company, stumbled across the odd new company and loved it. They partnered with Eyler and began handing out car mustaches at meetings, conferences, and tradeshows. They also gave them as gifts to investors. Eventually, they put big pink versions of the Carstache on the front of most of their vehicles and hired Eyler to help them with brand experience.

The pink mustaches worked because they made *Lyft* vehicles stand out and got everyone talking. People wanted to know why there were cars with big fuzzy mustaches on the grill. The mustaches also gave *Lyft* a reputation for being fun, whimsical, and irreverent.

In an Inc. magazine article, Christine Lagorio-Chafkin explains *Lyft's* choice of pink for the car mustaches and their overall brand.

> The bright pink color was inspired not only by the founders' desire to seem friendly and bold, but also to make their branding a bit less masculine than competitors, and nod to their very welcome view toward female passengers and drivers, as well as emphasis on safety for women.

And *Lyft* isn't the only company that understands the combined power of pink and vehicles. In 2016, David had the opportunity to speak at Nurse Next Door's annual conference in Vancouver. The theme was Bold Pink. It couldn't have been a more perfect fit.

The company provides senior home health services and they set themselves apart by their use of distinctive bright pink cars that go from home to home. They developed a technique called *parketing*, a portmanteau for parking and marketing. Unwilling to buy billboards as a scrappy startup, Nurse Next Door would instead park their pink branded vehicles in high traffic areas to generate awareness. What a great example of micro-weirding.

Their unique approach attracted new franchisees, new employees, and new clients. Their CEO, Cathy Thorpe, believes that pink and parketing are representative of their disruptive approach to the industry.

The M in F.L.A.W.S.O.M.E. is for Micro-weirding, tiny oddities. Now, let's look at the last letter in the framework: Exposing.

CHAPTER 13

EXPOSING

"Follow the path of the unsafe, independent thinker.
Expose your ideas to the danger of controversy.
Speak your mind and fear less the label of 'crackpot'
than the stigma of conformity."

— Thomas J. Watson, Jr.

"Honesty and transparency make you vulnerable.
Be honest and transparent anyway."

— Mother Teresa

"A lack of transparency results in distrust
and a deep sense of insecurity."

— Dalai Lama

Exposing is about honesty, transparency, and authenticity. It is a prerequisite for everything we've talked about so far. In order to create a Pink Goldfish, you have to be willing to reveal, instead of conceal; declare, instead of deny; disclose, instead of disguise; confide, instead of hide. You need a foundation of truth, which is uncommon in a world of spin control and subjectivity.

This suggestion either seems obvious or ridiculous. It's obvious that integrity and honesty are important. Almost every company includes something along those lines as one of their core values. But very few companies actually live up to those values.

On the other hand, it can seem naive and idealistic, maybe even unrealistic, to believe that companies should be honest in a hyper-competitive and litigious business environment. This chapter opened with quotes by Mother Teresa and the Dalai Lama extolling the virtues of transparency. But as respected as these two icons are, they might not seem like role models for successful marketing or business strategy.

But being open and honest today is a differentiator. As George Orwell, author of *1984*, once said, "in a time of universal deceit — telling the truth is a revolutionary act." In other words, when everyone else is lying, you can distinguish your brand simply by being honest. Exposing is a powerful tool for standing out.

We want to take a moment to practice what we preach. David loves this Orwell quote and he has used it in another book and in his presentations. But as we were updating Pink Goldfish, we did a little research and discovered that, although George Orwell might have written or said something similar, there is no evidence that this quote is his.

At that point, we had a decision to make. We could include the quote and hope no one finds out that the quote isn't legitimate. We could take the quote out. Or we could use the quote and be honest about its disputed origins. As you can see, we chose the last option. Hopefully, this demonstrates, in a small way, the effectiveness of exposing.

Exposing sits in the SUBTRACT quadrant in the bottom left of the matrix:

Simon Mainwaring is a brand futurist, author, and CEO of We First, a creative consultancy. He agrees with the Dalai Lama, Mother Teresa, and George Orwell, writing that "the keys to brand success are self-definition, transparency, authenticity, and accountability." So let's take a look at the power of being straightforward and candid, especially when the traditional approach to marketing involves highlighting positive features, and repairing or obscuring any negative ones.

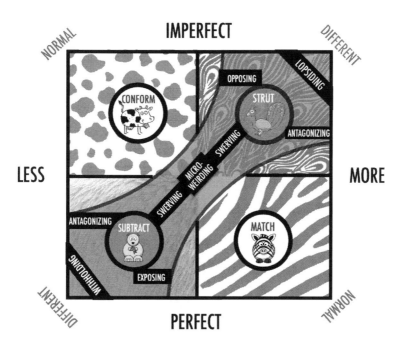

The message on a bag of Domino sugar explains that "Sugar is a 100 percent natural simple carbohydrate. Carbohydrates are an important part of any balanced diet. Sugar contains no fat or cholesterol and has 15 calories per teaspoon." They make it sound like the perfect food.

Domino's strategy seems to make sense. Why would you want to tell potential customers about what's wrong with your stuff? It seems foolish. And that is why very few companies do it.

However, there's a major problem with this approach. We all know that sugar isn't the perfect food and that undermines our ability to trust Domino. They aren't being honest.

We know that nothing is perfect. Pretending that your stuff is flawless hurts your brand. In contrast, acknowledging that your stuff isn't perfect makes it easier to love your brand.

According to Chip and Dan Heath, authors of *Made to Stick*, openly admitting limitations helps us build trust. This is true when discussing our own limitations or those of our ideas, products, or services.

"We've all come across salespeople who are reluctant to admit any weakness in their product or service, no matter how insignificant. As many a sales guru has pointed out, building trust involves being candid, and being candid involves admitting that your products aren't flawless. Admitting weakness can, oddly enough, make your core ideas more powerful."

Similarly, brand consultant Vicki Stirling believes that "admitting mistakes and flaws are actually really good tools to encourage loyalty."

IT'SUGAR is a great example of Exposing and they approach sugar much differently than Domino. Instead of trying to pretend that sugar is healthy, they put all of the negatives right on the label.

IT'SUGAR is a candy store that was founded in Atlantic City in 2006. Since then they've expanded to 100 locations nationwide. Honesty starts with their name.

What do they sell? Sugar. What's the main ingredient? Sugar. They sell Gummy Bears the size of your head. They sell a Gummy Worm that weighs three pounds. They sell Nerds in family-size cereal boxes.

The first time David visited one of their stores, he was traveling with his daughter for a keynote speech in New Jersey. They saw the store on the boardwalk and had to go inside. Since then, he has taken each of his daughters to that same store. His entire family has visited the store in Myrtle Beach.

The packaging on their giant chocolate bar illustrates the essence of exposing. In huge letters, it says. . .

> HIGH CHOLESTEROL
> GMOs
> NON-ORGANIC
> 100% SUGAR
> ARTIFICIAL FLAVORINGS
> NO ANTIOXIDANTS
> 100% GLUTEN
> EXTRA FAT

Are you willing to be that forthcoming about your products and services?

Speaking of sugar, it's time for a road trip to the middle of the country and the middle of the corn belt, the source of all that high-fructose corn syrup in our sweet treats. We are headed to Nebraska.

Nebraska isn't for everyone - Imagine that it's your job to get people to visit Nebraska. You want them to spend money and limited vacation days on a trip to your state. That's a real job at Nebraska Tourism. What would you do? How would you convince people to check it out?

From 2014 to 2018, the tourism slogan for Nebraska Tourism was "Visit Nebraska. Visit Nice." Did you ever hear anything about that campaign? Have you ever visited Nebraska? Do you know anyone who has? It doesn't count if you drove through on your way to someplace else, and that's a real challenge. Colorado is just to the west. Whitewater rapids. 14,000-foot Rocky Mountain peaks. The Olympic Training Center in Boulder. How does Nebraska compete with that?

South Dakota is right above them. The Badlands. Mount Rushmore. The Sturgis Motorcycle Rally.

What does Nebraska have? The Corn Palace. We'll give you a minute to Google it.

But they're not just competing with neighboring states. They're competing with any destination in the rest of the United States and the world. Broadway and Times Square in New York City. The Great Barrier Reef in Australia. Safaris in Africa. Carnival in Rio. The Great Wall of China. Penguins in Antarctica. The Leaning Tower of Pisa in Italy. Disneyworld. Disneyland....

There's one more thing you should know. For four years, Nebraska was ranked last as a tourist destination in the United States. Out of 50 states, the other 49 were more popular than Nebraska.

We don't know about you, but we wouldn't take the job. It seems like an impossible task. Here's how most cities and states do it. They promote what they have and act like it's better than it really is. They focus on the positive and ignore everything else. They also use some variation of "we've got something for everyone in (enter your state here)."

But this isn't a hypothetical scenario. John Ricks took the job. He agreed to be Nebraska's tourism director and Ricks and his team came up with something new in late 2018. Here's their new slogan, "Nebraska. Honestly, it's not for everyone."

Photo Credit: Nebraska Tourism

Instantly, everyone was talking about Nebraska. That's not much of an exaggeration. Stephen Colbert devoted an entire monologue on *The Late Show* to Nebraska's new tourism slogan. He concluded by asking Nebraska if they were OK. Nebraska Tourism responded brilliantly on *Twitter.* "No, we're not OK... That's Oklahoma."

In addition to newspapers, magazines, and radio programs, like *NPR's All Things Considered*, Nebraska was also featured on the *Today Show* and *Live with Kelly and Ryan*. Ricks estimates that the campaign earned them about $5 million in free publicity. Even more importantly, they've seen a 300 percent increase in traffic to their website and a similar increase in requests for travel guides.

Nebraska. Honestly, it's not for everyone. Honesty, it works.

Sometimes a Pink Goldfish isn't for everyone.

Snowbird and one-star reviews - "Too Advanced" and "Disappointed." These are a couple of the one-star reviews that were part of a genius marketing campaign by Snowbird. The mountain resort in Utah knows that they are not for every skier and snowboarder. The trails at the mountain are difficult. Some may see that as a flaw or weakness, but it's a badge they wear with pride.

In a brilliant example of exposing, they decided to display their bad reviews, instead of hiding them.

★☆☆☆☆   NO EASY RUNS
"We felt like our lives were in our own hands."
Jeremiah, Manchester NH

★☆☆☆☆   DISAPPOINTED
"Are the people who operate the grooming equipment on strike or something?
Was hoping for a little more corduroy to put my skis into."
— Elizabeth, Dallas TX

★☆☆☆☆ TOO ADVANCED
"I heard Snowbird is a tough mountain, but this is ridiculous. It felt like every trail was a steep chute or littered with tree wells. How is anyone supposed to ride that? Not fun!"
— Greg, Los Angeles CA

In the words of Gerald Weinberg, "If you can't fix it, feature it." Take pride in your unique characteristics. Emphasize them, expose them, and openly display them like Snowbird.

Sometimes a Pink Goldfish is a one-star ski resort.

Lochhead owns the haters - Christopher Lochhead is the founder of the *Follow Your Different* podcast, co-author of *Niche Down* and *Play Bigger*, and co-creator of *Category Pirates*. The first line of his *LinkedIn* bio is "Over-rated. - podcast review" The background picture on his profile includes three more negative reviews.

"Off-putting to some."
"Uses profanity needlessly."
"Very disappointing."

It doesn't stop there. In late April 2021, Lochhead explained on *LinkedIn* why he was going to "waste" his money promoting negative reviews of his podcast in *Podcast Magazine*. This time he added two new gems. "Jarring to the listener" and "Annoying host."

- It's funny
- It's different
- It's provocative
- It's a first in podcasting
- Knowing who is NOT your customer, is more important than knowing who IS your customer

This is classic exposing. He isn't trying to hide negative reviews. He's not trying to get them removed from online platforms. He's not trying to spin them or explain them or apologize for them. He's using them as a screening tool, to attract the right listeners and repel the wrong ones.

Sometimes a Pink Goldfish is very disappointing.

> "As I talk to clients who have been upset by negative reviews & haters, I often drop the line, 'Your brand is often defined by the people who hate you.' It inspires people who might otherwise have been indifferent to see what all the fuss is about. When people find out the hatred is unwarranted, they stick around to defend & love you."
>
> — Laura Bergells, corporate trainer and online educator

Unrating Vienna - "Paintings are disgusting." This was the one-star (★☆☆☆☆) review posted by Toby M. of the Leopold Museum in Vienna. Instead of hiding this review or disputing it, Vienna's Tourist Board projected the negative review on the side of the museum by the Vienna Tourist Board.

This was part of a campaign entitled "Unrating Vienna" in 2019. The goal was to highlight bad, yet funny, reviews in hopes of convincing people to see Vienna for themselves before forming an opinion.

Norbert Kettner, the Tourist Board CEO shared some background on the reasoning to *Lonely Planet,*

> We take a humorous look at the notion that online ratings are not always the right path to take when it comes to looking for relaxation and moments of enjoyment. The campaign is intended to make people sit up and think and trigger broader public discussion.

Sometimes a Pink Goldfish is a disgusting painting.

Dove's campaign for real beauty - One of the main goals of Dove's campaign for real beauty was to display images of real women of all shapes and sizes, instead of just including retouched photos of tall and thin models. They exposed scars and wrinkles and curves and blemishes that are usually absent from advertising campaigns. They deliberately sought out short women and tall women, old women and young women, big women and small women, and women of different races and skin tones and hair colors.

Their mission was to change society's narrow definition of beauty and to expand it to include a wider range of characteristics. Instead of pushing women to conform to an unrealistic and unattainable standard of attractiveness, Dove wanted women to feel accepted and appreciated just as they are.

And they didn't just expose the real appearance of real women. They also exposed the practices of the media and the beauty products industry that seek to present a one-sided and one-dimensional image of attractiveness.

Dove is a Unilever brand. In March 2021, Unilever made the move to remove the word "NORMAL" from all of its beauty products. The maker of Lifebuoy, Axe, Sunsilk, and Dove is attempting to usher in a new era of beauty that is more equitable and inclusive.

The initiative is called "Positive Beauty." A 10,000-person, nine-country study commissioned by Unilever found that 7 in 10 people agree that using the word normal on product packaging and advertising has a negative impact. For those aged 18-35, it rises to 8 in 10. Nearly three out of four people want to see the beauty and personal care industry focusing more on making people feel better than just looking better. Unilever is Exposing in an effort to better "challenge narrow beauty ideals."

Exposing is effective. In 2020, the Dove brand was valued at approximately $5 billion, increasing about ten percent compared to the previous year. Their Real Beauty Sketches won 19 Awards at Cannes Lions International Advertising Festival. The Campaign for Real Beauty was awarded the Grand EFFIE and also won Best US Campaign of the past 20 years.

Sometimes a Pink Goldfish has scars, blemishes, and wrinkles.

Facing up to aging - Justine Bateman released a new book in 2021 entitled *FACE: One Square Foot of Skin*. Bateman shared her goal for the book to Yahoo, "I hope that for all women, they could just look into what's making them think they need to change this one square foot of skin."

Justine is now 55. She burst into the mainstream at age 16 in the hit TV series *Family Ties*. She recalls in the introduction of the book how she admired the European actresses as a teen:

> I really wanted to look like the older European actresses I saw in the 1960s and '70s. Chiseled cheeks...dark circles...loose skin on the jawline...crow's feet. To me, these facial markings were the hallmarks of complex and exotic women with confidence and attitude and style.

At age 40, Bateman googled her name and read the comments. Somehow not having plastic surgery had become a negative. It affected her.

FACE shares 47 short stories about older faces and challenges the idea that those faces need to be fixed. "Once you read those reasons, most of them outdated... and based in fear, it will become difficult to continue to hold that erroneous idea any longer. Because there's nothing wrong with your face."

Bateman prompts us to embrace the idea of exposing, "What would happen if we just continued to become more and more and more ourselves?"

Sometimes a Pink Goldfish doesn't get plastic surgery.

PERSONAL BRANDING PROFILE

Ashley Graham is a big success. In 2016, the model became the first plus-size model to appear on the cover of the Swimsuit Issue for *Sports Illustrated*.

Graham is five feet, nine inches (175 cm) tall and weighs over 200 pounds. She is not afraid of exposing who she is. She recently shared with the *New York Post* that she's never felt uncomfortable with her shape.

Growing up, Graham was a size 12 by age 12. "I was always beyond confident because my mom and dad never put me down for my size." She is a tireless advocate for body positivity. "Let's face it, America is getting bigger, and women want to see themselves instead of the image of what society says they should be."

Throughout her career Graham has always been open about her experiences as a model. In 2017, Graham released her memoir, *A New Model: What Confidence, Beauty, and Power Really Look Like.*

Continued...

@AshleyGraham currently has 12.6 million followers on *Instagram*, where she regularly uses #BeautyBeyondSize to promote new attitudes towards weight and attractiveness. She also exposed her experience with pregnancy and its effects on her body, as well as posting photos of herself breastfeeding her new baby.

She doesn't just practice exposing. She encourages her followers to do the same. In a recent post, she asked her fans to share their favorite part of their body. She said her thighs are "the strongest part of her body," and that she wouldn't change anything about her body.

She argues that she's not hot for a big girl. She's just hot. She didn't always believe this. During her childhood, she struggled with dyslexia and kids who called her "thunder thighs."

One of her recent projects is for the plus-sized fashion brand, Lane Bryant. The campaign is called #ImNoAngel, which is a not-so-subtle shot at Victoria's Secret.

PINK PROFILE

"Pink is always shocking and naked."

— Derek Jarman, British film director

Valerie Steele, author of *Pink: The History of a Punk, Pretty, Powerful Color*, believes that pink is a symbol of "nakedness and vulnerability." These qualities are the essence of exposing. Nakedness is the ultimate transparency. Nothing is hidden. And vulnerability is about revealing weakness and imperfection.

Steele's view is supported by Barbara Nemeitz. In her book, *Pink: The Exposed Color in Contemporary Culture*, she says that pink is "revealing." She goes on to suggest that pink is also about sensitivity, calling it "one of the most important emotional qualities we associate with pink."

Nemeitz also argues that those who use pink in their work are "taking a position." Pink enables you to stand out by taking a stand. Instead of hiding who you are or what you believe or how you operate, you expose it.

It's almost time to talk about how to bring your Pink Goldfish to life, but before we do that, we need to address a question you've probably been asking since you started reading this book and we began extolling the virtues of being unashamed and unapologetic. Are there times when companies should apologize? Are there times when companies shouldn't flaunt or antagonize?

If you want to argue that there are times when Flaunting and Antagonizing are not the right strategy, you are absolutely right. Flaunting and Antagonizing are both about being unapologetic. However, there are certainly times when a company should apologize. Here is a quick reference guide for when to apologize and when to flaunt and antagonize.

Antagonize when a customer complains about something you *intentionally* don't provide.

Apologize when a customer complains about something you *unintentionally* failed to provide.

Antagonize when you are criticized for being *intentionally* different.

Apologize when you are criticized for being *unintentionally* ineffective.

Here are company examples from each part of the FLAWSOME framework that clarify this important distinction.

Flaunting
Buckley's shouldn't apologize for cough syrup that tastes terrible.
They should apologize for broken bottles or missing safety seals.

Lopsiding
Hardee's shouldn't apologize for unhealthy and outrageous food.
They should apologize for getting your order wrong or having unsanitary restaurants.

Antagonizing
Alamo Drafthouse shouldn't apologize for their strict no-talking and no-texting policy.
They should apologize for dirty theaters or poor service.

Withholding
Jimmy John's shouldn't apologize for having a limited delivery area.
They should apologize if they fail to make good on their freaky fast delivery promise.

Swerving
Big Ass Fans shouldn't apologize for having mild profanity in their company name.
They should apologize for fans that malfunction or orders that arrive late.

Opposing

Tinder shouldn't apologize because their app doesn't help people find lasting love. They should apologize if their company engages in sexual harassment.

Micro-Weirding

Magic Castle Hotel shouldn't apologize for "small swimming pools and underwhelming room décor." They should apologize if the popsicle hotline doesn't work or if the popsicles are melted when they arrive.

Exposing

Nebraska shouldn't apologize for not being New York City or Colorado. They should apologize if they have a terrible tourism website or incorrect maps.

In other words, when you are doing something wrong *on purpose* or you are *deliberately* not doing something, you shouldn't apologize. You should flaunt and antagonize.

On the other hand, when you do something wrong *accidentally* or you *accidentally* fail to do something, you should apologize. You shouldn't flaunt or antagonize.

Our goal for this section was to help you understand what FLAWSOME means. Our goal for the next section is to help you become FLAWSOME. Now that you know what FLAWSOME is, we want to show you how to create your own FLAWSOME business.

SIX A'S (THE HOW)

CHAPTER 14

BECOMING F.L.A.W.S.O.M.E.

A scene from Season 4, Episode 7

The Man in the High Castle

YUKIKO

"I have something for you."

Yukiko presents Robert a vase with golden seams.

"I repaired it while you slept. Using the kintsugi method,
lacquer mixed with powdered gold."

Robert holds the vase and admires it.

ROBERT

"Oh, Yukiko."

YUKIKO

"I know you can't sell it anymore,
but the anemones were too pretty to throw away."

ROBERT

"No, it's... it's wabi-sabi, you know.
Nothing lasts, nothing's finished, nothing's perfect."

We shared categories of examples showing WHAT companies have done to differentiate themselves in the previous FLAWSOME sections.

This section explores HOW to apply these lessons in your organization. We want you to go beyond kintsugi, which is simply illuminating existing imperfection, to wabi-sabi, which is creating intentional imperfection.

WABI-SABI

David had just finished presenting Pink Goldfish for the first time, when Patrick Ellis came up to talk with him after the keynote. Patrick is Canadian. He lives in Vancouver, British Columbia and he imports liquor. His specialty is sake and he has a profound understanding of Japanese culture.

He said he loved the explanation of Kintsugi and wondered if David had heard of Wabi-sabi. When David shook his head, Patrick leaned in and shared the fantastic concept.

Wabi-sabi is hard to explain and there are a lot of interpretations. Our explanation won't be perfect, but that's kind of the point.

Wabi-sabi is a combination of two old Japanese words with overlapping definitions. Grounded in the Buddhist view that both life and art are beautiful, not because they are perfect and eternal, but, because they are imperfect and fleeting. It is a design aesthetic of intentional imperfection.

Wabi-sabi is based on the belief that nature is beautiful and nature is imperfect. Therefore, we can make objects that are beautiful without needing to make them perfectly. Furthermore, we can make them imperfect on purpose. It's not a mistake. It's not incompetence. It's not poor quality control. It's a completely different standard, a completely different goal.

"In the East, in Japan particularly, the notion of Wabi-Sabi- the precious nature of the marred, imperfect, impermanent, and incomplete is an aesthetic norm. Easier to feel than to sum up. A notion, a sentiment or an impulse which commingles the materially terrible with the sublime. This emotion, this feeling, does not have the stern condemnation of the Western Memento Mori and it is not the fruit of guilt or denial. Just the serene embrace of the forces of creation and destruction that commingle in nature."

— Guillermo del Toro

Wabi-sabi is different from Kintsugi. It's not highlighting a pre-existing imperfection. It's creating intentional imperfection.

For example, pottery in the Wabi-sabi style might have a deliberate nick or scratch added right before it is fired. This same technique can be used in gardens or architecture. The final product might be asymmetrical or seemingly unfinished.

A modern example is the fascination with reclaimed wood from old houses, barns, and even pallets. The wood is used in furniture and on walls and in decorations because it is imperfect, not because people are unable to find new wood that is free of imperfections. The resulting creations are necessarily imperfect because they are made from damaged materials.

Sometimes it's easier to understand what something is by explaining what it isn't. A photoshopped image of a model isn't Wabi-sabi. It's an attempt to eliminate all imperfections. It is an attempt to improve on a flawed natural body. It is a false projection of an ideal. It is based on a belief that beauty and perfection are one in the same, that beauty is perfection and, by default, imperfection is ugly and disgusting.

Josh Burdett shared how intentional imperfection is practiced in Native American, Amish, and Persian cultures. Here is an excerpt from a post on the site *Conversations for Change:*[36]

There are Native American tribes who intentionally put mistakes in their artwork. While these purposeful imperfections have different intentions and meanings according to the tribe and the craft, they all believe the flaw to be important and necessary. The intentional error as an expression of humility is considered a way to honor the Great Spirit and to acknowledge being human.

It is not just Native Americans who include the practice of purposeful imperfection in their art. Persian rug weavers and Amish quilt makers are two other groups who employ similar policies in their craft. In addition to the expression of humility and honor, Persian rug weavers believe that mistakes also allow them to be more productive as they do not slow down their progress with needless worry, and that such freedom allows them to continually improve their skill. They support the paradox that practicing imperfection can allow you closer to perfection.

---

36. http://www.conversationsforchange.com/monthly-tidbits/april-tidbit-the-importance-of-mistakes

Here is another example that's close to home. When David designed a T-shirt to wear on stage, he wanted to make sure it was different. So he put the word "FREAK" upside-down on the shirt. It was Wabi-sabi, before he knew the concept. David did it incorrectly on purpose. It gets a lot of attention. People are always coming up and telling him that his shirt is upside-down. That is the power of Wabi-sabi.

Photo Credit: David Rendall

By the way, when he's wearing the upside-down freak shirt, the words look right-side up to him. As he looks down on his own shirt, it's a completely different perspective. This next example takes perspective to the next level.

Ray Bartkus is a street artist in New York. He created a unique mural in Marijampole, Lithuania on the Sesup River, by painting everything upside-down. It's called *Floating World*. Check it out at raybartkus.com.

But that's not the whole story. Because he painted the mural upside-down next to a river, when you look directly at the painting, it's upside-down, but when you look at its reflection in the river, it's right-side-up.

Photo Credit: raybartkus.com

The swimmers, swans, boats, and divers look out of place on the side of the building, but they make perfect sense on the surface of the water. Intentional imperfection. Deliberate differentiation.

David's T-shirt and Ray's mural are both examples of Opposing, which we discussed in Chapter 11. One way to do things wrong on purpose is to simply do the opposite of what everyone else is doing in your business or industry. When everything is right-side-up, just make something upside-down.

Now, imagine that you are a professor at Harvard University. You want to offer a new course to help students communicate more effectively. What do you call it? How will you get students interested? How will you communicate the content and value of the course? There are thousands of courses offered at Harvard each semester. How will yours stand out?

This isn't a hypothetical scenario. Alison Wood Brooks is an associate professor of business administration at Harvard. She is an expert in the psychology of conversation and she had a new course designed to help students get better at talking with each other.

So what did she call it? She called it *How to Talk Gooder in Business and in Life*. What?!? Gooder isn't even a real word. Why would a class at a prestigious university about how to speak well have a deliberate grammatical error in the title?

So what happened? Did anyone sign up for the brand-new class with an incorrect title? Yes, indeed. So many students, nearly 1,000, signed up and the class was full almost immediately. This is an elective course. No one has to take it. Professor Brooks needed to do something different if she wanted anyone to even know that the class was being offered. So she did. She used bad grammar to teach people how to talk gooder to each other.

IKEA has another great example of Wabi-sabi. They have repeatedly re-designed the Bang mug since its creation in 1996. One change is that each mug has a small chip at the bottom. This looks like damage, but it is done for a practical reason that also makes the mugs memorable.

The little circular chip is known as a "drainage gate." The practical purpose is to eliminate dishwasher residue on the bottom. According to the IKEA website, "the drainage gates on the underside transport water away that may otherwise accumulate when the mug is upside down in the dishwasher." In other words, this small little chip prevents that gross dishwasher puddle from collecting on the bottom of your mug.

Photo Credit: Stan Phelps

Ray Bartkus, Amanda Wood Brooks, and IKEA are all great examples of Wabi-sabi. They deliberately created something imperfect in order to differentiate. We want to show you HOW to do the same.

In the next six chapters, we'll look at how you can *reinterpret* your organization's strengths and weaknesses, *reinvent* your brand, and *reinforce* your reputation in order to stand out from your competition.

Reinterpretation involves Assessing (Chapter 15) and Appreciating (Chapter 16) your organization's flaws.

Reinvention includes Amplifying (Chapter 17) those flaws, then Aligning (Chapter 18) them with the right people, products, places, positioning.

Reinforcement is about Augmenting (Chapter 19) by combining strategies and Attacking (Chapter 20) the competition.

Let's start with Assess.

ASSESS

*"It's up to each of us alone to figure out
who we are, who we are not,
and to act more or less consistently with those conclusions."*

— Tom Peters

WHAT MAKES YOUR ORGANIZATION UNIQUE?

Being unique is about being different, being unusual, and being uncommon. Unfortunately, instead of embracing our uniqueness, we often try to hide it in an effort to be more normal. We tend to focus on the ways our businesses are similar to others. We've learned that benchmarking and emulating the success of other organizations is a proven path to success.

Because of this bias, it's helpful to spend some time thinking about what makes your company odd, atypical, and exceptional. We need to reinterpret who we are.

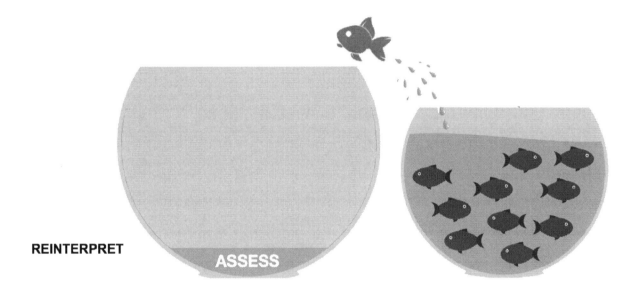

REINTERPRET

ASSESS

To help with this process, we've designed a simple checklist of possible company characteristics.

Almost every strategic planning process begins with an analysis of the organization's strengths, weaknesses, opportunities, and threats (SWOT). We've designed an organizational assessment to help you see your organization's strengths and weaknesses in a new light.

TAKE THE ASSESSMENT

Put an X in the box on the left next to the positive characteristics of your organization, people, culture, and products & services.

1. If you notice any characteristics that are definitely not a strength, draw a line through them.

2. Choose your organization's top five strengths out of the following 40 attributes and rank them from one to five (one being the strongest).

X	STRENGTHS	RANK
	1) agile, responsive	
	2) responsive, quick	
	3) spontaneous, instinctive	
	4) fast-growing	
	5) vigilant, alert	
	6) cooperative, friendly	
	7) sensitive, caring	
	8) personal, individualized	
	9) fun, entertaining	
	10) extravagant, generous	
	11) intricate, elaborate	
	12) unusual, exotic	
	13) hand-crafted, unique	
	14) exciting, high-performance	
	15) luxurious, sophisticated	
	16) audacious, courageous	
	17) new, innovative	

X	STRENGTHS	RANK
	18) revolutionary, activist	
	19) bold, daring	
	20) diversified, unlimited	
	21) systematic, organized	
	22) large, substantial	
	23) patient, deliberate	
	24) steady, stable-growth	
	25) satisfied, content	
	26) competitive, assertive	
	27) objective, rational	
	28) automated, programmed	
	29) serious, professional	
	30) frugal, thrifty	
	31) simple, clean	
	32) familiar, well-known	
	33) standardized, uniform	
	34) reliable, consistent	
	35) inexpensive, affordable	
	36) cautious, careful	
	37) established, reputable	
	38) classic, traditional	
	39) conservative, refined	
	40) focused, specialized	

Now, let's identify your organization's weaknesses:

1. Put an X in the box on the left next to the negative characteristics of your organization, people, culture, and products & services.

2. If you notice any characteristics that are definitely not a weakness, draw a line through them.

3. Choose your organization's top five weaknesses and rank them from one to five (one being the weakest).

X	WEAKNESSES	RANK
	1) reactive, unpredictable	
	2) small, weak	
	3) impatient, impulsive	
	4) unstable, volatile	
	5) unsatisfied, discontented	
	6) passive, reactive	
	7) vulnerable, emotional	
	8) labor-intensive, unpredictable	
	9) silly, immature	
	10) wasteful, reckless	
	11) complex	
	12) foreign, unfamiliar	
	13) irregular, rough	
	14) unreliable, inconsistent	
	15) expensive, over-priced	
	16) careless, foolish	
	17) untested, unproven	

X	WEAKNESSES	RANK
	18) rebellious, radical	
	19) irreverent, offensive	
	20) unfocused, scattered	
	21) bureaucratic, inflexible	
	22) bulky, cumbersome	
	23) slow, indecisive	
	24) slow, plodding	
	25) complacent, ignorant	
	26) aggressive, hostile	
	27) detached, insensitive	
	28) impersonal, cold	
	29) somber, humorless	
	30) stingy, cheap	
	31) plain, dull	
	32) regular, ordinary	
	33) ordinary, common	
	34) boring, predictable	
	35) cheap, low-quality	
	36) fearful, timid	
	37) old, outdated	
	38) old-fashioned, conformist	
	39) boring, uninspiring	
	40) limited, restricted	

NOW WHAT?

At this point, after completing the assessment of your organization's strengths and weaknesses, most business books would encourage you to use your newfound awareness to fix the weaknesses.

That's the exact opposite of what we're going to recommend. We don't want you to fix your weaknesses. We want you to appreciate them by discovering that your organization's weaknesses are important clues to your organization's most powerful strengths. Appreciation is the focus of the next chapter.

PERSONAL BRANDING PROFILE

Dav Pilkey is the award-winning and best-selling author of the *Captain Underpants* series of children's books, but his road to success wasn't easy. He explains his story succinctly in the About the Author section of his books.

> When Dav Pilkey was a kid, he suffered from ADHD, dyslexia, and behavioural problems. Dav was so disruptive in class that his teachers made him sit out in the hall every day. Fortunately, Dav loved to draw and make up stories. He spent his time in the hallway creating his own original comic books.
>
> In the second grade, Dav Pilkey created a comic book about a superhero named *Captain Underpants*. His teacher ripped it up and told him he couldn't spend the rest of his life making silly books.
>
> Fortunately, Dav was not a very good listener.

Even as an adult, Dav is still encountering obstacles. His books have been banned from libraries and elementary schools for being insensitive and/or inappropriate for specific age groups. Parents and teachers don't like the way his books encourage children to reject authority.

His name is an interesting example of micro-weirdness. He worked at Pizza Hut and the E was missing from his nametag. So he went with it and re-branded himself as Dav, instead of Dave. Although he still pronounces it the same way.

CHAPTER 16

APPRECIATE

"For there is nothing either good or bad,
but thinking makes it so."

— Shakespeare, *Hamlet*

Once you know your company's strengths and weaknesses, what should you do next? The conventional wisdom is to build on strengths and fix weaknesses. Don't appreciate what makes you different. Instead, adjust and adapt.

As you already know, we disagree with this approach because every weakness has a corresponding strength. So, let's build on the weaknesses instead. However, it only makes sense to do that if we reinterpret our organization's identity and truly appreciate the value of our organization's flaws.

Appreciation is the second part of reinterpreting.

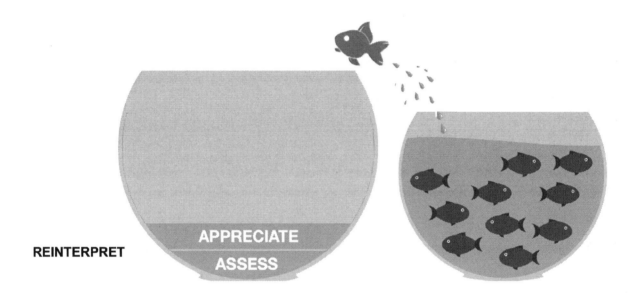

REINTERPRET

APPRECIATE

ASSESS

Appreciation is the essence of this book. We want to show you that your organization's flaws can make it awesome, but that can be very difficult in an environment that provides more criticism than appreciation.

Within our organizations, most of us are more familiar with criticism than appreciation, especially when it comes to being unusual. As Alex Bogusky warns, "Life conspires to beat the rebel out of you."

Because of this external pressure to conform and to homogenize our organization's offerings, most companies try to find a way that pleases everyone or displeases no one. But it simply isn't possible to find an approach that makes all customers happy. Anything we do will end up alienating someone. We demonstrated this specifically in the chapter on Antagonizing. If we believe that our company can please everyone by becoming perfect, by fixing all of our weaknesses, we will fail. For example, not everyone likes Starbucks or McDonald's or Apple or Walmart, and yet they are very successful companies.

Our company's products or services can't make everyone happy, and it is futile to try. Frances Frei and Anne Morriss, in *Uncommon Service*, encourage managers to "decide what trade-offs you will make—where you will do things badly, even very badly, in the service of being great....Dare to be bad. We think there is nobility in the attempt to be good at everything, but that effort only leads to exhausted mediocrity." Success is about delighting the right customers and being willing to make other customers unhappy.

A second major barrier to appreciating our organization's flaws is comparison. When it comes to competition, it is tempting to compare our organization to others that seem more successful or more popular. We imagine that they have big strengths and no weaknesses. But this isn't true.

As we'll see in this chapter, our organization's apparent weaknesses are also strengths, and the competition's obvious strengths are also weaknesses. We need to find ways to capitalize on our organization's unique characteristics and use our apparent flaws to our advantage.

A great example of appreciation, and a lack thereof, can be found in the discount retail industry. Let's start with Walmart. Their main strength is low prices, but their weaknesses include poor quality merchandise, long lines, and unhelpful employees.

What would happen if, instead of appreciating their flaws, Walmart tried to fix their weaknesses? What would happen to their low prices, their primary strength, as they added better products and extra employees at the registers? The answer is simple. Their prices would climb, thus diminishing their strength.

Walmart isn't accidentally bad at service, quality, and design. They are deliberately weak in those areas so they can maintain their strength of low prices. Regardless of whether you like their strategy, it is working. Walmart has more than 11,000 stores and 2.2 million employees in 26 countries. They are also the largest grocery retailer in the United States with a profit of more than $14 billion in 2020.

Meanwhile, one of Walmart's primary competitors is Target. Their main strengths are higher quality products from well-known designers, attractive stores, and helpful associates who are quick to open a new checkout lane. However, Target's main weakness is that their prices are not as low as Walmart's.

What if Target decided to fix their weakness by lowering prices? What would happen to the level of customer service and the great products that give them their advantage, if they focused more on cost cutting? Again, the answer is clear. Their quality and service would decrease, thus diminishing their strength.

"Since its founding, it (Target) has intended to differentiate its stores from its competitors by offering what it believes is more upscale, trend-forward merchandise at lower costs, rather than the traditional concept of focusing on low-priced goods." This strategy is paying off. The median household income of Target's customer base is roughly $64,000, much higher than the incomes of Walmart's customer base. They are ranked #37 on the *Fortune* 500 list of US corporations by total revenue and they had a profit of almost $3 billion in 2019.

At this point, you might be skeptical. Can't companies be well-rounded and balanced and successful? To answer this question, let's look at Kmart. They provide an illustration of what happens when a company doesn't practice appreciation and tries to fix weaknesses, instead of focusing on strengths. Their historical leadership in discount retail was based on the blue-light special, a symbol of low prices. Kmart was "The Savings Place." However, when faced with competition from Walmart, they did not focus exclusively on this price advantage and began to lose customers.

Kmart then began adding designer products from celebrities like Martha Stewart, but wasn't quite ready to shed their low-price image. This allowed Target to capture higher-income customers who were design-conscious, while Walmart attracted lower-income customers who were cost-conscious.

Kmart's efforts to fix their weaknesses ultimately led to bankruptcy. They became undifferentiated. They weren't the best at anything, so customers had no reason to shop there. Their failure illustrates the dangers of trying to eliminate weaknesses and be more well-rounded. As Harvard marketing professor Youngme Moon explains in her book, *Different*, "True differentiation is rarely a function of well-roundedness; it is typically a function of lopsidedness."

There is a compelling reason to go to Walmart—low prices. There is a compelling reason to go to Target—better service and design. But there is no compelling reason to go to Kmart. Their prices aren't the lowest and their service and design aren't the best. In their effort to become well-balanced and well-rounded, they became average, mediocre, and invisible.

And it keeps getting worse. After going bankrupt, Kmart bought Sears. Neither company made significant changes to their strategies and the combined company went bankrupt again, closing stores throughout the country. In their attempt to be the best of both worlds, they became the worst of both worlds.

This is crucial. When we try to fix organizational weaknesses, we often end up damaging the corresponding strengths. Our efforts to make our companies better can end up making them worse.

As Frances Frei and Anne Morriss explain in *Uncommon Service*, "striving for all-around excellence leads directly to mediocrity."

It may seem like reinterpreting and appreciating is just denial, dishonesty, or spin control, but they're not. Each business has unique characteristics that have both positive and negative features. These features, which we usually refer to as strengths and weaknesses, cannot be separated. They come in pairs. The positive and negative elements are inextricably linked.

It's common to believe that there's nothing strong about your particular weaknesses or the weaknesses of other businesses. However, every weakness has a corresponding strength.

For example, consider Republic Wireless. The Raleigh-based company provides a value-based mobile phone service that costs just $20 a month. They aren't flashy and they don't try to be. They are "boring" by design. Isn't boring a bad thing? Not necessarily.

Another billboard promises "A monthly bill as expected as Capital Blvd traffic." There are no surprises when you get your statement.

Boring means reliable and predictable. Their weakness is also a strength.

Republic Wireless also frames their customers' weaknesses as strengths. They claim to be "The best mobile carrier for ~~penny pinchers~~ the fiscally conservative."

Now let's look at the connections between your organization's particular strengths and weaknesses.

Transfer the top five strengths and top five weaknesses from the last chapter to the chart below.

	STRENGTHS		WEAKNESSES	
			High Adaptablity	
EXAMPLE	**Flexible**		*Low Structure*	
Zara	1) agile, responsive	☐	1) reactive, unpredictable	☐
Startups	2) responsive, quick	☐	2) small, weak	☐
Tesla	3) spontaneous, instinctive	☐	3) impatient, impulsive	☐
Bitcoin	4) fast-growing	☐	4) unstable, volatile	☐
Intel	5) vigilant, alert	☐	5) unsatisfied, discontented	☐
	Friendly		*Low Discipline*	
EXAMPLE			*High Connection*	
Planet Fitness	6) cooperative, friendly	☐	6) passive, reactive	☐
Zappos	7) sensitive, caring	☐	7) vulnerable, emotional	☐
Nurse Next Door	8) personal, individualized	☐	8) labor-intensive, unpredictable	☐
Tom's Diner	9) fun, entertaining	☐	9) silly, immature	☐
Magic Castle	10) extravagant, generous	☐	10) wasteful, reckless	☐
			Low Consistency	
EXAMPLE	**Weird**		*High Variability*	
Cheesecake Factory	11) intricate, elaborate	☐	11) complex	☐
Trader Joe's	12) unusual, exotic	☐	12) foreign, unfamiliar	☐
Sam Adams	13) hand-crafted, unique	☐	13) irregular, rough	☐
Jaguar, Snowbird	14) exciting, high-performance	☐	14) unreliable, inconsistent	☐
Prada	15) luxurious, sophisticated	☐	15) expensive, over-priced	☐
			Low Caution	
EXAMPLE	**Wild**		*High Innovation*	
Hardees	16) audacious, courageous	☐	16) careless, foolish	☐
Kickstarter	17) new, innovative	☐	17) untested, unproven	☐
Patagonia	18) revolutionary, activist	☐	18) rebellious, radical	☐
Shinesty	19) bold, daring	☐	19) irreverent, offensive	☐
Buc-ees	20) diversified, unlimited	☐	20) unfocused, scattered	☐

STRENGTHS	WEAKNESSES	
Low Adaptability *(italic)* **High Structure**	**Linear**	**EXAMPLE**
21) systematic, organized ☐	21) bureaucratic, inflexible ☐	NASA
22) large, substantial ☐	22) bulky, cumbersome ☐	Budweiser
23) patient, deliberate ☐	23) slow, indecisive ☐	United Airlines
24) steady, stable-growth ☐	24) slow, plodding ☐	Chick-fil-A
25) satisfied, content ☐	25) complacent, ignorant ☐	Westvleteren
High Discipline **Low Connection**	**Logical**	**EXAMPLE**
26) competitive, assertive ☐	26) aggressive, hostile ☐	Crossfit
27) objective, rational ☐	27) detached, insensitive ☐	BVG
28) automated, programmed ☐	28) impersonal, cold ☐	Woot
29) serious, professional ☐	29) somber, humorless ☐	IRS
30) frugal, thrifty ☐	30) stingy, cheap ☐	Republic Wireless
High Consistency **Low Variability**	**Accepted**	**EXAMPLE**
31) simple, clean ☐	31) plain, dull ☐	Minecraft
32) familiar, well-known ☐	32) regular, ordinary ☐	Velcro
33) standardized, uniform ☐	33) ordinary, common ☐	McDonald's
34) reliable, consistent ☐	34) boring, predictable ☐	IBM
35) inexpensive, affordable ☐	35) cheap, low-quality ☐	IKEA
High Caution **Low Innovation**	**Accessible**	**EXAMPLE**
36) cautious, careful ☐	36) fearful, timid ☐	Procter & Gamble
37) established, reputable ☐	37) old, outdated ☐	eHarmony
38) classic, traditional ☐	38) old-fashioned, conformist ☐	Listerine
39) conservative, refined ☐	39) boring, uninspiring ☐	Nebraska
40) focused, specialized ☐	40) limited, restricted ☐	In-N-Out Burger

Look for connections between strengths and weaknesses. For example...

- Companies can be seen *negatively* as small and weak (2) or *positively* as quick and responsive (2)
- Services can be seen negatively as complex (11) or positively as intricate and elaborate (11)
- Products can be seen negatively as overpriced (15) or positively as luxurious (15)

> *"When you choose anything, you reject everything else.... So when you take one course of action, you give up all the other courses."*
>
> *— G.K. Chesterton*

PERSONAL BRANDING PROFILE

Paul grew up in a hard-working, middle-class family in Southern California. In second grade, he still didn't know the alphabet. Efforts by his teachers, parents, and siblings didn't seem to help. He was eventually diagnosed with both dyslexia and ADHD (Attention Deficit Hyperactivity Disorder). After failing a few grades and being expelled from several schools, he finally graduated from high school with a 1.2 grade point average and a ranking of 1,482 out of 1,500 students.

Based on his disability and poor performance in school, most people wouldn't have predicted success for Paul. In fact, Paul himself was often concerned that he would end up homeless. He started a small business selling school supplies and copies in a store so small that he had to move the copier out to the sidewalk. The business eventually grew to 1,200 locations in ten different countries and, in 2004, Paul Orfalea sold Kinko's to FedEx for more than $2 billion.

How did a dyslexic guy who can't read or write build such a successful business? Orfalea argues that he succeeded because of his disability, not in spite of it. Because of his weaknesses, he had to trust others and rely on them to help him run the business. For example, he needed people to assist him with correspondence. This evolved into a culture of teamwork and collaboration that separated Kinko's from their competitors. Paul hired people who were strong where he was weak.

Because he was restless, he spent most of his time out of his office and in the stores, observing the practices of frontline employees. Because he was impulsive, he quickly implemented new ideas throughout the organization. His intuitive intelligence and racing mind made him impatient and easily frustrated, but many employees credit these traits with creating a sense of urgency that motivated people to make changes and improvements.

Orfalea wrote *Copy This! Lessons from a Hyperactive Dyslexic Who Turned a Bright Idea into One of America's Best Companies* with journalist Ann Marsh, but because of his dyslexia, he's never been able to read his own book. In it, he credits his disabilities for his success and says he thinks everyone should have dyslexia and ADHD. During his many speaking engagements, he advises audiences to "like yourself, not despite your flaws and so-called deficits, but because of them."

Paul Orfalea didn't just appreciate his own weaknesses; he also created an organization that appreciated the weaknesses of its employees. He turned Kinko's into a Pink Goldfish by demonstrating sensitivity for the limitations of others, such as stubbornness, impatience, disorganization, and impulsiveness. Since he wasn't perfect, he didn't expect perfection from others. He readily admitted his own flaws and accepted the flaws of his employees. Because he couldn't do everything well and relied on others to complete essential tasks, he also allowed others to find team members that complemented their weaknesses.

Additionally, he wasn't afraid to be different, and he encouraged his employees to approach their work in unique and creative ways. This created a culture of innovation, trust, and teamwork that made Kinko's a perennial favorite on *Fortune's* 100 Best Companies to Work For.

"Once you've accepted your flaws, no one can use them against you."

- Peter Dinklage

Instead of trying to create perfect organizations, we need to appreciate our company's limitations and make sure that we don't let what we cannot do interfere with what we can do.

(DIS)OWNING YOUR FLAWS

To appreciate your flaws requires you to fully accept them. You can't back down in the face of criticism or public pressure. Let's look at a number of brands who suffered commitment issues:

Kimpton kills their pink goldfish - InterContinental Hotels Group (IHG), one of the largest hotel companies, acquired Kimpton in December 2014. In 2018, IHG made the move to discontinue the Guppy Love program as a result of complaints from PETA (People for the Ethical Treatment of Animals).

According to *USA Today*, Faith Yi, a spokeswoman for Kimpton remarked, "We partnered with PETA to humanely re-home the goldfish from the handful of properties where the Guppy Love program was active."[37] Yi shared that Kimpton will "find other creative ways to delight our animal-loving guests and we remain as pet-friendly as ever."

This hurts Stan's feelings because Kimpton was the foundational example of his goldfish book series. Kimpton did not consult Stan before making this decision.

South Dakota quits Meth - In 2019 the South Dakota Department of Social Services launched a public health campaign entitled, "Meth - We're On It." It was an effort to bring South Dakotans together to fight the raging meth crisis in the state. This "double meaning" campaign took over the airwaves and the internet, creating a huge amount of exposure. The State and Governor Kristi Noem faced a lot of public criticism and social media ridicule because of the campaign and this caused them to hit the brakes on the tagline.

A year later they were still backpedaling, Secretary of Department of Social Services, Laurie Gill shared, "Meth We're On It' is what we used in our first awareness campaign and we're pivoting now to 'Anyone Everywhere,' the whole idea here is that meth can be used by anyone in South Dakota and it can happen anywhere. It doesn't matter if you live in rural South Dakota or in the urban areas."

We think this is a missed opportunity. Everyone was paying attention to their first campaign. That is rare for a public health initiative. They should have taken advantage of that attention. They should have been unapologetic. Instead, they apologized and backed down. It is unlikely that anyone either knows or cares about their new and improved campaign. This is because, in their effort to make it right or good or better, they made it so bland that it was invisible.

Burger King's Unhappy Meals - In 2019, the fast-food chain introduced a range of boxed deals called "Real Meals." The swipe at the McDonald's Happy Meal included five varieties: the Pissed Meal, the Blue Meal, the Salty Meal, the YAAAS Meal, and the DGAF (Don't Give a F*ck) Meal. The limited time offer was tied into Mental Health Awareness Month. Each Real Meal included a Whopper, fries, and a drink.

In a joint announcement, Mental Health America CEO Paul Gionfriddo shared, "Burger King is bringing much-needed awareness to this important and critical discussion – and letting its customers know that is OK to not be OK." The launch featured a print advertisement showing a montage of people in various emotional states, using the line: "No one is happy all the time. And that's OK."[38]

37 https://www.usatoday.com/story/travel/roadwarriorvoices/2018/01/16/no-more-fish-kimpton-eliminates-room-aquariums/1037172001/

38. https://www.mashed.com/152027/twitter-reacts-to-burger-kings-unhappy-meals/?utm_campaign=clip

Not everyone was thrilled with the campaign. For example, the co-founder of *The Daily Wire* Ben Shapiro commented, "This is a hell of an ad for depression eating." As with South Dakota, there was widespread criticism in the traditional press and on social media so Burger King eliminated the Real Meals.

We think that, if there is a criticism of the program, it's the limited way Burger King executed it. They should have ramped up the meals, instead of cutting them. The Real Meals were only available at five restaurants. They could be purchased in Seattle, New York City, Los Angeles, Austin, and Miami Beach, but only at specific stores.

We would have loved to see them make this a permanent offering. McDonald's offers Happy Meals, Burger King could have given you permission to be unhappy, at every restaurant, every day.

Frontier grounds the Britney promotion - In February 2021, Frontier Airlines ran a social media promotion. The airline announced on *Twitter* that anyone with the first name "Britney" was eligible to fly for free.

Frontier used the hashtag #FreeBritney in reference to the singer, Britney Spears, and her efforts to end her conservatorship. Since 2008, a conservatorship has limited the control Britney has over her finances. Her father controversially serves as a co-conservator. The topic was made more public and more relevant with the recent release of the documentary *The New York Times Presents Framing Britney Spears* on *Hulu* and *FX*.

This opportunistic approach used by Frontier is called "newsjacking." David Meerman Scott wrote an entire book on the concept, which uses current events as a platform for promoting a company's products or services.

Frontier Airlines faced a significant backlash to the offer. In response, they deleted the tweet, ended the promotion, and went radio silent.

Should they have stuck with it? Perhaps they had the best interests of Britney in mind. But given the lack of response, it was probably more of a stunt. In the words of David Meerman Scott, "Probably best to avoid trying to sell something off the news of somebody else's misfortune."

We think they could have made it work if they had just framed it as supporting Britney Spears specifically, by helping Britneys in general. They had an opportunity and they missed it. They could have flaunted it. Instead, they apologized.

Tesla makes a smashing debut - In November 2019, Tesla revealed the first version of its Cybertruck. The futuristic vehicle looks like something out of the movies. During the unveiling, a man with a sledgehammer hit the sides of the truck without damaging it. Impressive. But a subsequent demonstration of the truck's supposedly unbreakable glass windows backfired when a metal ball thrown at the window smashed it. Undaunted, they threw another metal ball at another window. Smash! That one broke as well.

Photo Credit: *YouTube*

Elon Musk was unfazed. He did the remainder of the introduction with the two broken windows. The next day he tweeted a response about the glass, "Sledgehammer impact on door cracked base of glass, which is why the steel ball didn't bounce off. Should have done steel ball on window, *then* sledgehammer the door. Next time…"

A few months later Tesla announced the sale of a commemorative T-shirt. According to their site, the Cybertruck Bulletproof Tee is "Designed for exceptional comfort and inspired by the Cybertruck unveil event, the Cybertruck Bulletproof Tee is made from 100% cotton and features our signature Cybertruck icon on the back."

As with the other examples we've shared in this section, there was a huge backlash in the media regarding the broken windows and the failed test. Many commentators saw the unveiling as a mistake and predicted that the Cybertruck would be rejected by customers. It would have been easy for Tesla to apologize or cover up, but they didn't. They flaunted it. They drew even more attention to it. They made a T-shirt about it.

Tesla also got 650,000 pre-orders, at $100 each, for the truck, which earned them $65,000,000.[39] Maybe the shattered windows created even more attention than if the unveiling had gone perfectly. Maybe the event was FLAWSOME. Maybe they broke the windows on purpose.

Unlike Kimpton, South Dakota, Burger King, and Frontier - Tesla has doubled down on imperfection. If you can't fix it, flaunt it.

One way to deal more effectively with public criticism is to reframe it as a sign that you are doing something right. Sally Hogshead, author of *Fascinate*, argues that "It's okay to have a few people hate your brand. In fact, it's necessary. If you're not eliciting a negative response from someone, then you're probably not very compelling to anyone." Being criticized, by at least some potential customers, means you are on the right track. In this way, criticism becomes a form of positive feedback or praise.

We've now completed the first two A's of Assess and Appreciate. Once you've Reinterpreted your strengths and weaknesses, it's time to Reinvent your organization by finding or creating Alignment.

---

39. https://www.inputmag.com/culture/tesla-has-more-cybertruck-pre-orders-than-the-number-of-cars-its-delivered-in-two-years

CHAPTER 17

ALIGN

"People don't know what they want until you show it to them."

— Steve Jobs

Most of this book has been about being different; this section is about similarity. It's time to find people who are weird like you, who have the same weaknesses or who like your style. It's time to move to places where your flaws fit in and where your products are perfect. Aligning is matching, connecting, and linking your organization's uniqueness with the people, both internally and externally, who value that distinctiveness.

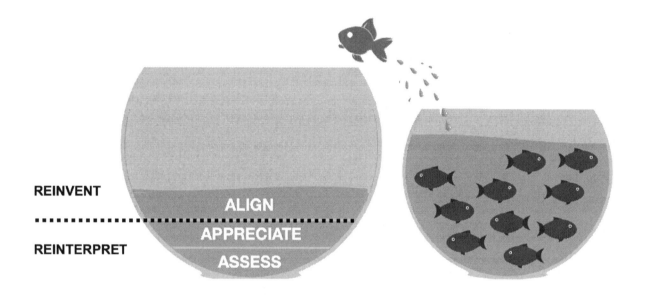

Let's start with ugly fruit and deformed vegetables.

Each year millions of people struggle with hunger and food insecurity and each year millions of pounds of healthy and nourishing food is wasted. There are many reasons that food either spoils or is destroyed before it can be sold or used.

The first reason is just appearance. Odd or misshapen fruits and vegetables are rejected by grocery stores and, because of this, are usually destroyed or left to spoil by farmers.

Second, some foods are not the right size or shape for a specific use so they can't be sold to a company to be used as an ingredient.

Third, sometimes farmers have too much of a particular item and there isn't enough demand for it.

Fourth, when a company creates new packaging for a product, they stop selling the product in the outdated packaging. These food products are often disposed of, even though there is nothing wrong with the contents, just the packaging.

Finally, some food can't be sold to stores because they don't want to stock items that are too close to their expiration date. To be clear, they haven't expired, but the store only wants items that are a specified amount of time (like three months) from their expiration dates.

This is where Imperfect Foods comes in. They are on a mission to "eliminate food waste and build a better food system for everyone." They purchase, organize, package, and sell a lot of the food that no one else will buy or sell.

As they explain on their website, "If food can be saved, we will save it. With every bite into a misshapen apple, short piece of pasta, or oversized egg we can shape our world for the better. We're hungry for change and eager to reduce waste on the farm, at the store, and in the home."

We love the way they talk about their work. They've "rescued" 139 million pounds of imperfect food. They have over 300,000 "imperfect" customers and 1,500 "imperfect" employees. Their imperfect company has sales of over $400 million and they won the Modern Retail Award in 2020.

One of their core values is "Be Imperfect." In their words:

> We believe what's different about us is worth celebrating. We understand that personal and team growth only happens if you bring your whole, authentic self to work and are excited to learn from mistakes. We embrace the intersection of compassion and accountability.

Perfectly Imperfect Produce in Cleveland, Ohio has a similar mission. They encourage customers to "rethink perfect." They believe that "the true beauty of a fruit or vegetable is how it nourishes your soul."

Both of these companies do a great job of aligning with three groups of customers:

- people who value sustainability and want to reduce food waste
- people who are on a budget and want to reduce their food costs
- people who want to eat fresh and healthy fruits and vegetables

Alignment is crucial. As Seth Godin constantly argues, "Everyone is not your customer." The FLAWSOME strategies only work when they match the needs of specific groups of customers. Now let's see what happens when a company fails to align their strategy with their customers.

Ron Johnson misunderstood the value of alignment during his 17-month stint as CEO at JCPenney. The former Target and Apple executive failed so spectacularly that he might have destroyed the company he was hired to save.

Mark Cohen, a former CEO of Sears Canada, described Johnson's work this way. "There is nothing good to say about what he's done...JCPenney had been run into a ditch when he took it over. But, rather than getting it back on the road, he's essentially set it on fire."

Probably his biggest error was Johnson's focus on eliminating sales and discounts. He did this in a department store with a reputation for big markdowns and customers who really liked to feel like they were getting a great deal. Unfortunately, his strategy was not aligned with what JCPenney customers valued.

"I thought people were just tired of coupons and all this stuff," Johnson told *Businessweek*. "The reality is all of the couponing we did, there were a certain part of the customers that loved that. They gravitated to stores that competed that way. So our core customer, I think, was much more dependent and enjoyed coupons more than I understood."[40]

The idea of alignment might seem obvious, but it might not be as clear how or why customers might want flawed products or services. So here are some examples of how companies' unique imperfections align with the people they are trying to serve.

Flaunting

Buckley's can flaunt the terrible taste of their cough syrup because there are people who believe that bad taste is evidence of a medicine's effectiveness. If it doesn't hurt, it's probably not working.

Mini can flaunt the small size of their cars because there are people who dislike big gas guzzling SUVs and value small fuel-efficient vehicles.

Lopsiding

Hardee's can sell high-fat and high-calorie foods because there are people who want tasty and filling food at a low price.

Antagonizing

Alamo Drafthouse Cinema can antagonize people who talk or text during movies because there are people who want to enjoy a movie without distractions.

Withholding

Chick-fil-A can be closed on Sundays because there are people who value family time and work/life balance.

---

40. https://www.bloomberg.com/news/articles/2013-01-29/ron-johnson-acknowledges-j-dot-c-dot-penney-isn-t-apple#r=lr-fs

Swerving

REI can be closed on Black Friday because they have customers who value outdoor activities more than shopping.

Opposing

Patagonia can buy back used clothing, clean and repair it, and then resell it as "Worn Wear" because their customers are also serious about sustainability and environmental responsibility. Their goal is to create products that last longer and are replaced less often, but they need to align with customers to make this vision a reality.

Micro-Weirding

The Magic Castle Hotel can succeed with simple rooms, a small pool, and basic decorations because some people really love free popsicles and snacks.

Exposing

Dove can put real women with real flaws in their commercials because most of us have flaws and we are happy to finally be represented.

Snowbird's one-star advertisements work because they repel the untrained and casual skiers and attract the experienced and thrill-seeking skiers.

Alignment requires a fit between the organization and its customers, but that process doesn't always start with understanding customers. Sometimes it starts with understanding and clarifying your organization's values and identity. Sometimes the right customers find you because you're living out your values.

Borzou Azabdaftari is the Iranian-American founder of NickelBronx, a creative agency in Washington, DC. David met Borzou at a series of workshops they both attended a few years ago. Borzou's story of turning his company values into customer alignment is perfect for this chapter. We asked him to tell the story in his own words.

> I wish I could tell you the evolution of our marketing was more strategic. It was born from an attempt to be authentic, but also from an inability to describe what we do in a concise elevator pitch.
>
> What do we do? We make cool shit.
>
> I guess it started when I realized our core values were bullshit. I learned about core values in the Entrepreneurs' Organization's (EO) Accelerator program, and I think

I picked some things that sounded nice like "Truth, Justice, and the American way." Not that, but something like that. After a few years of holding onto them and trying to make my employees care about things I didn't care about, we redid them.

The first one, which eventually became our tagline and really secondary logo - was "Make Cool Shit." Why? Not just that we make things that are cool - but we endeavor to make everything cool. If it was cool last time, how could it be better next time? Cool is a moving target, it changes, it gets better. That's what we wanted to focus on.

Core values are typically for staff, not all companies have them outward-facing. We really liked "Make Cool Shit" though. We couldn't help ourselves. First, we made them as koozies for a tailgate event we sponsored. This was mostly a younger crowd, and we figured it would be fine there, so we weren't really surprised people liked it. Then, we made T-shirts, but again just for the staff. It was still our thing, for the inner circle. Even customers we let in on it were told to keep it quiet. We really just didn't know how people would react.

Little by little it leaked out though. More and more people wanted a shirt, or a koozie. People started saying they were coming here to make cool shit. It meant something to our customers. Without explanation or effort, it meant the same thing it did to them that it did to us. It was really special.

You're supposed to vet customers by your core values first, and nothing does that better than tossing a curse word in it. Honestly, if (the word) shit bothers you that much, you're probably not going to get through a meeting with me anyway. It catches people's eye, and if I'm honest, the graphic is just awesome, and people are drawn to it. We get requests from all over the country. I really need to start selling our apparel. People can relate to it, to us.

Have there been bumps? Sure, but very few from actual customers. I had a lady at the grocery store yell "good thing he can't read" about my two-year-old, and I didn't say anything. But I thought, "he's two. Why the fuck would he be able to read?" It occurred to me later that she said this because he was wearing a "Make Cool Shit" shirt.

I've had one good customer ask me not to send them anything that says shit on it, and not to use stuff we've printed for them in our social media because curse words are off brand for them, which I totally respect and understand.

However, I also heard a story about a meeting where the marketing team for a $200 billion company was reviewing our creative and the Vice President saw our Make Cool Shit and was taken aback, saying "wait what kind of company is this," to which someone replied, "they're edgy - we need that."

Is cussing still edgy? I don't know. You can search *Amazon's* best sellers list and find a ton of books about how many fucks you should give. It works for us because it's real. One of our other core values is "Give a Fuck." A mentor told me I could have just used "care." I told him he can have everyone who cares. I want the people who give a fuck.

Swearing is a way to attract people who align with your approach and repel the people who don't. Look no further than Gary Vaynerchuk and Christopher Lochhead, the books *Go the F*ck to Sleep* and *The Subtle Art of Not Giving A F*ck*, or rated R movies and MA video games.

PERSONAL BRANDING PROFILE

Celebrity chef Rachel Ray doesn't mind being criticized, because she knows that not everyone is in alignment with her mission and message. "If you spend so much time thinking about the people who dislike what it is you're doing, you're doing a disservice to the people that employ you. I'm not employed by those people. I work for the people that want the type of food I write [about], the type of food we share with people."

An unconventional brand strategy requires unconventional customers to buy your product or service. If flaws make your brand awesome, then maybe flaws make your customers awesome. Are you looking for strange shoppers, crazy consumers, and unusual users?

Alignment is essential because being a Pink Goldfish is only effective if you discover customers who want more of what you do well and who don't care about what you don't do well. According to Frei and Morriss in *Uncommon Service*, "Excellence requires underperforming on the things your customers value least, so you can over-deliver on the dimensions they value most."

IKEA is a great example. They underperform AND over-deliver. Most furniture stores have salespeople who help you choose high quality, expensive furniture that will last for a very long time. You might be able to pass it along to your children. Once you commit to the purchase, your selections will be delivered to your home and assembled for you.

IKEA is purposely unlike an ordinary furniture store. Compared to traditional furniture stores, IKEA underperforms. They have a lot of weaknesses. They don't have salespeople, and it's hard to find what you need as you wander through their gigantic warehouse. They don't have high-quality furniture. It isn't expensive. It won't last for generations. They won't deliver it. You have to assemble it.

It's easy to see how IKEA underperforms, but it's hard to see how they over-deliver. This is crucial. They discovered that many customers saw traditional furniture store's strengths as weaknesses and that those same customers saw IKEA's weaknesses as strengths.

For example, salespeople can be helpful but they can also make customers feel uncomfortable and pressured. IKEA doesn't pressure you.

Purchasing lifetime furniture is expensive and a big commitment. IKEA furniture is inexpensive so it isn't a big commitment. You can just replace it when it goes out of style or breaks.

Furniture delivery takes days and sometimes weeks. Furniture from IKEA goes home with you today.

Traditional furniture is assembled for you. When you assemble your IKEA furniture, even though the process is frustrating, you have a sense of accomplishment from being involved in the process. This feeling is so powerful, and seemingly universal, that it has been confirmed in repeated research studies. It is called the IKEA effect.

The IKEA effect is that people value things more when they are involved, at least somewhat, in the process of making those things. In fact, people overvalue what they have made even when it is compared to a superior object made by someone else. For example, when someone has built, or customized, their home, they consistently set the price too high when it comes time to sell.

IKEA discovered what customers value most and then over-delivered in those areas. They also discovered what customers valued least and underperformed in those areas. Their imperfect approach has been very effective. Since 2008, IKEA has been the world's largest furniture retailer with revenue above $45 billion in 2019 and a valuation of $18 billion. IKEA has also been recognized by *Forbes* as one of the best companies in the world to work for.

But maybe you don't want to build your own furniture, maybe you want to build your body.

CrossFit was founded by Greg Glassman and Lauren Jenai in 2000. It is promoted as more than just a method for working out. It is also a sport, a philosophy, and, for some, a religion. The goal of CrossFit is partially explained in its name. The workouts are designed to make participants fit in every major area such as muscular strength, cardiovascular capacity, and flexibility.

A CrossFit gym is called a "box" and there are more than 15,000 boxes in 150 countries around the world. Most of the boxes are intentionally rugged. They are very hot or very cold, depending on the weather. They are loud, dirty, and smelly. There are no shiny machines. Most aren't neatly organized.

While completing the WODs (workout of the day), people are sweating profusely, grunting, screaming, yelling, and sometimes crying. They are pushing their bodies to the brink. No one is wiping down machines or even their own bodies. It's a free-for-all. CrossFit members are also famous for being fanatical evangelists for this unique approach to exercise and life. If someone does CrossFit, they will talk about it in almost every conversation. They brag that their warm-up is harder than most other people's entire workout.

High-intensity interval training is a hallmark of CrossFit WODs. These workouts vary dramatically with the goal of achieving muscle confusion. Instead of consistent, routine, and programmed exercise, CrossFit attempts to stimulate fitness gains by challenging the body in surprising and unpredictable ways. CrossFit isn't for everyone. It isn't even for most healthy people who exercise regularly. It certainly isn't for people with a casual approach to exercise.

CrossFit's massive success led to the creation of the CrossFit Games, which are sponsored by Reebok. The winners of the event are crowned as the "fittest man on earth" and the "fittest woman on earth." Thousands of people compete around the world for a chance to participate in the games. Thousands more attend the multi-day event as spectators. *Netflix* has produced multiple documentaries of the games called "Fittest on Earth."

CrossFit is intentionally difficult. It is purposely extreme. It is about being bigger, better, faster, and stronger. That is what makes it so attractive and so energizing for some people. CrossFit doesn't need to make their WODs easier. They don't need to tone it down, ease up, or lower their standards. They go farther and appeal to people who want to go farther. And there are a lot of those people. CrossFit now operates in more than 15,000 locations worldwide. Their customers have turned CrossFit into a cult with more than $4 billion in annual revenue.

CrossFit is successful because they appeal to a specific type of person, but CrossFit isn't for everyone. Some people are looking for a completely different workout experience. That is where Planet Fitness comes in.

The Grondahl brothers started Planet Fitness in New Hampshire in 1992. Their differentiation strategy is to provide low-cost memberships and an accepting environment for people who are joining a gym for the first time or who only work out sporadically. In contrast to CrossFit boxes, Planet Fitness locations are full of very clean and neatly organized exercise machines. The environment is brightly lit and climate controlled. Never too hot. Never too cold.

Their advertising promotes Planet Fitness as a "no judgement zone," but that isn't really true. They won't judge you for being out of shape. They won't judge you for skipping workouts. They won't judge you for how you look or what you wear. But they will judge you if you're really fit, if you're really intense, or if you try really hard. If you grunt or breathe hard or slam the weights, they'll ask you to leave and not come back.

Planet Fitness is accepting if you have a dad bod or a muffin top, but they are antagonistic if you are a bodybuilder or musclehead. They deliberately and publicly exclude customers with those goals and habits. Their advertising campaigns openly ridicule people who are passionate about being strong and fit. Those ads simultaneously attract the customers Planet Fitness wants to serve while repelling the customers they want to exclude. Planet Fitness isn't ashamed of how they openly discriminate against hyper-fit people in order to help their members workout without intimidation or fear of being embarrassed. By the way, CrossFit enthusiasts refer to Planet Fitness as "Planet Fitless."

Planet Fitness is succeeding with their unique strategy. They have more than 2,000 locations and over 15 million members, which makes them one of the largest fitness club franchises. Their 2019 revenue was $689 million and *Newsweek* ranked them #2 on the List of America's Best Companies for Customer Service.

So how do you find alignment between your imperfections and your customers? Here are four questions that might help.

1. Which customers love you?
2. How can you create even deeper connections with them?
3. Which customers hate you?
4. How can you make them even more unhappy?

If you want to find weird employees and weird customers for your weird products, you might need to go to a weird place. Cities, towns, and communities are brands too. We've already discussed Nebraska, Vienna, South Dakota, and Kazakhstan. Let's look at some additional examples of locations that illustrate the importance of alignment.

One place that is famous for being weird is Austin, the capital of Texas. They are known around the world for their "Keep Austin Weird" campaign, which has defined the city for decades. But it's fair to ask a simple question. Does weird work? Absolutely. Let's look at the facts.

With a population of just over one million residents, Austin is the 10th largest US city. They have been rated as the best city in the US for jobs. They also have been the third fastest growing US city. They've been recognized as the best city for growing businesses, and Austin has been named as one of the top three travel hotspots.

But maybe it's easier to be weird when you're a big city and a state capital. What about a smaller city like Portland, Oregon, population 660,000? They've adopted the slogan "Keep Portland Weird." How are they doing?

Portland is also doing very well. They were ranked one of the top 10 best places to retire in the US. They are the second greenest city in the entire world. They are also the most bike-friendly city in the US and the second most liked city in the US.

But even though Portland is smaller than Austin, it isn't really a small city. Asheville, North Carolina, has a population of under 100,000, and they are trying to stay weird too. They like to say that "If you're too weird for Asheville, you're too weird."

Deanna Loew, an Asheville resident, proudly proclaims that Asheville is the strangest place you will ever visit and has the weirdest people in the country.

> Asheville has an eclectic mix of hippies, doctors, and southerners. We are smack dab in the middle of the Bible Belt, the Blue Ridge Parkway, and one of the biggest medical centers in the US. I consistently see a man with a purple mohawk hula-hooping in the middle of Pack Square in a tutu. When you go to the local grocery store, you are confronted with hippies, suburban housewives, doctors in scrubs, real life cowboys, and a vast array of other eclectic Ashevillians. I truly do not think that there will ever be a city more diverse than Asheville. We may be weird, but those who live in Asheville love this quirky little town. Yes, we are strange. Yes, we are proud. Yes, we are Asheville.

And weird is working. Asheville has been named the "New Freak Capital of the US." They are one of the top 10 places in the US to reinvent your life and one of the top 10 most beautiful places in the US. They are also one of the top 25 best places for businesses and careers in the country.

Weird works in America, but it also works globally. In 2014, Samari, Yamartino, and Davari compiled statistics on every country in the world to discover what each country was best at. Here are some of the highlights. This may help as you search for a place that wants what your brand creates.

Canada leads the world in maple syrup and asteroid impacts. If you're trying to sell artificial pancake syrup, you probably shouldn't do it in Canada. But if you're selling equipment for doomsday preppers, you might find a receptive market.

Australia is the leader in deadly animals and melanoma. There are a lot of ways to die in Australia. This might be a great market for sunscreen, health care services, or anxiety medication.

China is the highest in CO2 emissions and renewable energy. They are working both sides of that equation, creating and solving the pollution problem. If you provide emissions control systems, China is a potential customer. If you are in the renewable energy industry, China is a potential partner.

Greenland provides the most personal space. That's a positive way to say that no one lives there. It isn't a big market, but what do they do with all that space? Maybe you can sell them a fence or an ATV or some cows.

Russia has the most raspberries and nuclear warheads. There seem to be opportunities here for organic farmers and global arms dealers.

The Netherlands has the tallest people on earth. If your brand specializes in weird sizes, the Dutch need your help.

New Zealand is the best at rugby and sheep. Maybe you could sell them some wool uniforms.

The United States has the most lawnmower deaths and Nobel laureates. Apparently, we have both the dumbest and smartest people on Earth. Maybe you need to start researching some lawn mower safety innovations or better ways to cut the grass. You might be able to get some sheep from New Zealand.

There's an illusion that there is a perfect place with perfect customers and perfect employees, but there is no such thing as a perfect place.

For example, David moved from Wisconsin in the Midwest to North Carolina in the South. The weather is much warmer in North Carolina, and the winters are much milder than in Wisconsin, but it isn't perfect.

Wisconsin has harsh winters featuring extreme cold and blizzards, but it doesn't have hurricanes. However, Wisconsin does have tornadoes. If you try to avoid tornadoes and hurricanes, you'll likely end up in a place that has floods.

Southern California is known for its consistently warm temperatures, but it's also plagued by drought, mudslides, wildfires, and earthquakes. Colorado has beautiful mountains, but it also has avalanches, something you don't have to worry about in Kansas.

There's plenty of sunshine and warm temperatures in Phoenix, but it also has monstrous dust storms called haboobs.

Vancouver in British Columbia is a great illustration of how the weaknesses and strengths of a place are connected.

On the positive side, Vancouver

- is one of the most livable cities in the world.
- has the fourth highest quality of living on earth.
- is the tenth cleanest city on earth.
- has the fourth thinnest residents in Canada.

On the negative side, Vancouver also

- has the worst traffic congestion in Canada.
- has the second most unaffordable housing on earth.
- has one of the highest crime rates in North America.
- is the most densely populated Canadian city.

It's easy to see how some of the city's weaknesses are directly related to its strengths. Traffic congestion and unaffordable housing are due to the area's quality of life. Everyone wants to live there.

Additionally, Vancouver's dense population is both a positive and a negative. For sustainability experts and city planners, density is one measure of a city's success. However, if you're from Greenland and you're looking for some personal space, you're not going to find it in Vancouver.

As you build your Pink Goldfish, you need to assess, appreciate, and align. You need to match your weirdness and weakness with the right customers and communities. Once you are aligned, you can go even farther. It's time to own and exaggerate your apparent flaws. Let's move to the fourth A of Amplifi.

CHAPTER 18

AMPLIFI

*"My goal is to be weirder than everybody else
and hope that no one stops me.
So far, no one has."*

— Alexandra Petri,
humorist and newspaper columnist

mplifying is the essence of flaunting your weakness and weirdness. This is the act of not only shining a light on what makes you unique, but actually turning up the dial on your imperfections.

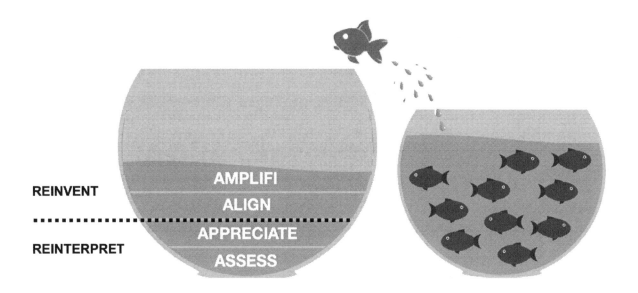

To steal a phrase from the rockumentary *This is Spinal Tap*, you should "turn it up to 11." In the movie, the lead guitarist, Nigel Tufnel, proudly demonstrates an amplifier whose knobs are marked from zero to eleven, instead of the usual zero to ten.

Photo Credit: Wikipedia Commons

In 2002, the phrase was entered into the *Shorter Oxford English Dictionary* with the definition "up to maximum volume." Here is the dialogue from the movie between Nigel and Marty DiBergi, the Director, played by Rob Reiner:

> **Nigel:** See. The numbers all go to eleven. Look, right across the board, eleven, eleven, eleven and...
>
> **Marty:** Oh, I see. And most amps go up to ten?
>
> **Nigel:** Exactly.
>
> **Marty:** Does that mean it's louder? Is it any louder?
>
> **Nigel:** Well, it's one louder, isn't it? It's not ten. You see, most blokes, you know, will be playing at ten. You're on ten here, all the way up, all the way up, all the way up, you're on ten on your guitar. Where can you go from there? Where?
>
> **Marty:** I don't know.
>
> **Nigel:** Nowhere. Exactly. What we do is, if we need that extra push over the cliff, you know what we do?
>
> **Marty:** Put it up to eleven.
>
> **Nigel:** Eleven. Exactly. One louder.
>
> **Marty:** Why don't you just make ten louder and make ten be the top number and make that a little louder? [Long Pause.]
>
> **Nigel:** These go to eleven.

To Amplifi isn't simply having awareness, knowing your strengths and weaknesses. It isn't just appreciation, valuing your strengths and weaknesses. To Amplifi is to get weirder by getting weaker.

There are two parts to the Amplifi process: maximizing and minimizing.

- Maximizing is spending MORE time, energy, and resources on what makes us imperfect.
- Minimizing is spending LESS time, energy, and resources conforming to traditional models of success.

MAXIMIZE

Mario Andretti is one of the most successful American drivers in the history of racing. What's the secret to his success? It's simple. Go faster. He is famous for saying that "if everything seems under control, you're not going fast enough."

As you create your own Pink Goldfish, people will tell you that you've gone too far. How should you respond? It's simple. Amplifi. Go even farther.

Marmite is a strong example of maximizing. It tastes awful and it's not for everyone. Marmite is brewer's yeast, a byproduct of the beer-making process. It was originally produced in England by the Marmite Food Extract Company in 1902. It is currently made by Unilever.

The product is concentrated into a thick brown paste that has a very strong flavor and an incredibly salty taste. It is usually spread thinly on bread or toast.

So is Marmite disgusting or delightful? Yes. It's both. Many consumers are devoted to it. Many others despise it.

To highlight Marmite's polarizing effect, the "*love it or hate it*" advertising campaign was created. It has been so successful that Marmite has become a metaphor in England for anything that evokes a strongly positive response from some and a strongly negative response from others.

Marmite is maximizing the offensively unique flavor of their product. They aren't trying to hide it or pretend it's delicious. They aren't trying to tone it down. They aren't creating a light version or a low salt version. In fact, they did the exact opposite.

In 2010, they introduced an extra-strength version, Marmite XO. If you thought Marmite was bad, they made it even worse. They decided that it wasn't too strong. It wasn't strong enough. This strategy worked beautifully and the first shipments sold out as soon as they landed on store shelves. Marmite embraced their fans and antagonized their haters. Marmite isn't for everyone.

Calling out the haters was a PR hit. Marmite saw sales increase by 60 percent at UK retailer Tesco and Unilever booked profits of more than $8 billion in 2018.

How could your organization apply the Amplifi strategy? Look back at your assessment results from Chapter 15. What are your organization's unique weaknesses? What if you maximized them? We're going to challenge you to take it "one louder."

Here are 11 sample questions and answers that might help:

1. **Are your products cheap? Make them cheaper.**
Some customers want the most inexpensive option, regardless of quality.

2. **Are your services too expensive? Increase the price.**
Some customers will see them as luxurious, lavish, or extravagant.

3. **Is your company boring? Make it even more dull.**
Some customers like to keep things simple or prefer a conservative approach.

4. **Are your products too complex? Make them even more confusing.**
Some customers will see them as intricate, sophisticated, and challenging.

5. **Is your service too impersonal? Remove people altogether.**
Some customers prefer automated systems.

6. **Is your company too serious? Become even more serious.**
Some customers will see you as professional, businesslike, and distinguished.

7. **Is your company too silly? Become even more ridiculous.**
Some customers will see you as irreverent and hilarious.

8. **Are your products too offensive? Make them even more shocking.**
Some customers want stuff that is bold and daring.

9. **Do you offer slow service? What if you made it even slower?**
Some customers enjoy the sense of anticipation.

10. **Are you failing to offer enough options? What if you offered even fewer?**
Some customers get overwhelmed with too many choices.

11. **Are you too cynical? What if you got even more pessimistic?**
Some customers will see it as realistic or satirical.

This is proven by the defeatists at *Despair.com*. They have turned negativity into a business by creating demotivational posters that parody the inspirational messages decorating corporate conference rooms across the country.

Here are some of our favorites:

QUALITY – The race for quality has no finish line—so technically, it's more like a death march.

TEAMWORK – A few harmless flakes working together can unleash an avalanche of destruction.

TEAMS – Together, we can do the work of one.

SYNERGY – A code word lazy people use when they want you to do all the work.

CUSTOMER CARE – If we really cared for the customer, we'd send them somewhere better.

CUSTOMER DISSERVICE – Because we're not satisfied until you're not satisfied.

APATHY – If we don't take care of the customer, maybe they'll stop bugging us.

MOTIVATION – If a pretty poster and a cute saying are all it takes to motivate you, you probably have a very easy job. The kind robots will be doing soon.

Maximizing is about spending MORE time, energy, and resources on what makes us weird and weak. Now let's focus on minimizing, which is about spending LESS time, energy, and resources conforming to traditional models of success.

MINIMIZE

As a transplant to the South from the Midwest, David enjoys the many new types of foliage. After several years, he is still amazed to see flowers bloom on bushes in early January. One very popular southern tree is the Crepe Myrtle. It caught his attention because of the way it is pruned. In the winter, you can see rows and rows of trees that have been cut back severely with only the largest branches remaining. This annual pruning maintains the health and appearance of the tree.

In our efforts to make our companies well-rounded and multi-faceted, we often develop branches that are unproductive. Unfortunately, we don't prune them and they end up sapping our strength.

Every company has a limited amount of time, energy, and resources. Minimizing (pruning) allows us to conserve those resources and use them in ways that improve our effectiveness.

Bo Burlingham profiles companies with a distaste for growth in his book, *Small Giants: Companies that Choose to be Great Instead of Big.* Anchor Brewing and Zingerman's are two of the small giants:

Anchor Brewing in San Francisco was in the middle of an IPO (Initial Public Offering). They were raising the necessary capital to fuel their growth when the owner, Fritz Maytag, decided that he didn't want to get bigger. They didn't continue with the IPO. As Maytag explained, "This is not going to be a giant company... on my watch."

Zingerman's Deli is another example from *Small Giants.* They are an institution in Ann Arbor, Michigan. Customers loved the food so much that nationwide expansion seemed like the obvious next step. They could have been the next McDonald's, Subway, or Chipotle. But they took a different approach and focused on their local area, creating Zingerman's Community of Businesses. Instead of getting bigger, they got better and helped other businesses get better as well with financial and management support. The deli and the other businesses earn more than $50 million per year.

> *"To fulfill some commitments, others must be excluded."*
>
> - Chris Guillebeau, *The Art of Non-Conformity*

Minimizing is unconventional, but it is a strategy with many advocates. Marcus Buckingham, author of *The One Thing You Need to Know*, argues that the most important thing to know about personal success is "if you don't like it, stop doing it." Peter Drucker, the father of modern management, encouraged companies to practice "organized abandonment." In *The Art of Non-Conformity*, Guillebeau refers to it as "radical exclusion."

Leadership guru Tom Peters recommends that you go a step further and get a "stop counselor" for your strategic planning meetings to help you eliminate unnecessary or distracting goals and activities. Jim Collins, author of *Good to Great*, argues that both businesses and individuals should create a stop-doing list. Here are a few tips from his website:

- Start an actual, physical list of things to stop doing.
- When you add a new activity to your to-do list, select an activity to stop doing.
- Rank your activities from most to least important. Drop the bottom 20 percent.
- Don't devote resources to activities that don't pass the preceding tests.

This is difficult advice because we're taught to be strong in all areas in order to succeed. Organizations experience intense pressure to moderate their unique characteristics instead of maximizing or minimizing them. Conventional wisdom says that our organizations should strive for perfection and balance. However, this isn't true. In fact, in order to be the best in one area, brands have to be willing to be the worst (or at least poor) in others.

For example, the two teams in the 2010 Super Bowl were the Indianapolis Colts and the New Orleans Saints. The Colts had the worst running game of any team in the NFL and the Saints had one of the worst defenses. However, the Colts also had one of the best passing offenses and the Saints made up for their poor defense with a league-leading offense. Both teams were the best in one area because they were the worst in another. Similarly, in 2013, the Seattle Seahawks won the Super Bowl. That same year, they were the most penalized team in the league.

PERSONAL BRANDING PROFILE

Matthias Schlitte offers an even more interesting example of this principle. He began practicing arm-wrestling when he was 16 years old but has only been training the muscles in his right arm. When you see a picture of him, it looks like he has some sort of genetic deformity and he does. It's called KTS, which causes one of a person's four limbs to grow much larger than the others.

His right forearm is nearly 18 inches (45cm) around, but his left forearm measures just 6 inches. It seems like the only muscles that he has are in his right arm. This is a huge advantage in arm wrestling because his opponents are determined by weight class. People wrestle against others of similar weight.

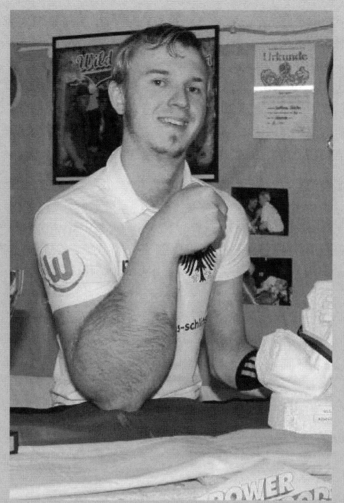

Photo Credit: Wikimedia Commons

Matthias' wrestling arm is much larger than that of his competitors because they have bodies with normal proportions. Unfortunately, this means that much of their weight is in parts of their bodies that don't help them with arm wrestling.

Schlitte can spend additional time and energy exercising his right arm (maximizing) because he doesn't have to bother with building the rest of his body (minimizing). He is weak in many areas so that he can be incredibly strong in the area that is the most important. This makes him unbalanced, but it also makes him successful.

We hope that you're ready to turn up the volume on your organization's weaknesses, but there's even more you can do to differentiate. You can combine more than one of the FLAWSOME strategies. We call this Augmenting and it's the beginning of Reinforcement.

CHAPTER 19

AUGMENT

*"If a little is great,
and a lot is better,
then way too much is just about right!"*

— Mae West

Each of the FLAWSOME strategies is powerful on its own, but they are even more powerful when they are combined. We call this augmenting. We don't want you to stop after implementing one approach. We want you to stack them, bundle them, link them, integrate them, blend them, fuse them, mix them, synthesize them, join them, and connect them.

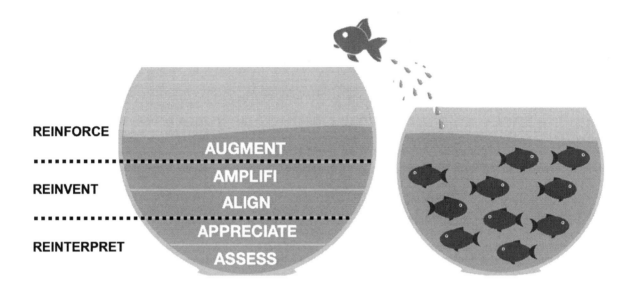

Does this sound too extreme or risky? Does it sound like a recipe for disaster? Probably. So let's take a look at this next example.

David fought Goliath and won. Well, that's not exactly true. Davide fought Yelp and won.

Let's start from the beginning. Davide Cerretini started Botto Bistro in Richmond, California in 2009, after losing his first restaurant in the 2008 financial crisis. Early on, he saw *Yelp* as an ally in his efforts to gain new customers, but that was going to change.

Why is *Yelp* so important? Research shows that even a ½-star improvement in an establishment's rating on *Yelp* can increase business by almost 20 percent during peak times. Davide was eager to earn positive reviews and see new faces walking through the doors of Botto Bistro, but that's not what happened.

Davide started to notice that five-star reviews from loyal customers were disappearing from *Yelp* and one-star reviews from questionable sources were multiplying. He contacted *Yelp* to find out what was happening, but was unable to resolve the issue. His suspicion was that *Yelp* was manipulating the reviews in an effort to convince him to buy ads on their platform. He isn't the first to complain about this tactic, but legal challenges from other businesses were unsuccessful.

So what did he do? After battling for five years, he reached a breaking point in September 2014. He was a small Italian restaurant with 10 tables at a single location. *Yelp* was a six-billion dollar publicly-traded company with a stock worth $94 per share. How could he fight back? How could he possibly win?

Most businesses just give in to the pressure. They purchase ads from *Yelp* and beg customers for good reviews. They do everything possible to please every customer and live in fear of the next negative review. They feel powerless to defend themselves. Not Davide. He didn't quit. Instead, he used a powerful combination of the FLAWSOME strategies to fight back.

As we explained earlier, Flaunting is the foundation of all the other strategies. Cerretini is a great example of this. He is definitely unashamed and unapologetic in the way he built his own majestic Pink Goldfish.

He started with Opposing.

Davide refused to play the game by the existing rules. He changed the game. He had a new goal. He didn't want high ratings. He wanted to be the lowest-rated restaurant on *Yelp*. He didn't want to be the best. He wanted to be the worst.

He made a simple offer. Receive 50 percent off your pizza if you post a one-star review on *Yelp*. Did it work? Yes. Immediately and beautifully.

He did more business in one day than he usually did in a month. He was also interviewed by the media from coast to coast, including: *Time, USA Today, The New York Times,* and *MSNBC.* Cerretini was also featured on *The Daily Show* and in a documentary about *Yelp.* Botto Bistro became a sensation.

This huge wave of attention didn't just help his restaurant. It became a galvanizing event for small businesses throughout the country. His opposition started a revolution.

Then he focused on Withholding.

Why did Botto Bistro get so many bad reviews in the early days? It was mainly because of all the things they don't do, and because they aren't the traditional American version of an Italian restaurant.

- No free bread
- No free olive oil
- No substitutions

- No pizza by the slice
- No ice
- No butter
- No ranch dressing
- No coupons
- No ambiance
- No servers
- No reservations
- No patience

Then he added big chunks of Antagonizing.

Botto Bistro's website featured a *Village Idiot* page with the *Top 10 Stupid Questions of the Month*. Here is a sample. . .

*   *   *

Any reference to any person or episode is not accidental.
We just don't know their names or we would definitely tell you.

Q. Do you guys have a kitchen here?
A. Yes (and you just made it to the top 10)

Q. Where are you from?
A. Italy.
Q. Did you actually live in Italy?
A. I'm Italian, I was born in Italy.
Q. But did you live in Italy?
A. No. My family and I took the first flight out of Italy right after I was born and never looked back.
Q. Oh I see.

Q. Can I ask you a stupid question? But I don't want to be posted on your newsletter with the stupid questions of the month.
A. Oh no don't worry that happens only to real idiots.
Q. Can the fettuccine Alfredo with chicken be made vegetarian?
A. (Ok, yes I totally lied! here you are).

(Looking with anger at our sign that says 'We have no ice, we have no butter')

Q. What kind of place has no ice and no butter?

A. This place.

Q. You really have no ice?

A. No.

Q. Really?

A. Actually we do, we have tons of ice but we love it so much that we want to keep all for ourselves, and we will not share with you. It is our precious.

Q. This is the worst place I have ever been to

Q. This place is supposed to be a Wing Stop.

A. Not since 2009.

Q. No way. I come here all the time.

A. If you are one of their best customers, now you know why they went out of business.

Q. I know you have a sign at the door saying 'No food or beverage allowed from outside' but can we bring our own wine?

A. No

Q. Why?

A. Because your wine falls in the category of beverages and it comes from the outside of this restaurant and anything included in the category of the beverages that come from outside of this restaurant is not allowed in this restaurant.

Q. Your sign should be more clear.

No matter where we are, Italy or United States, the village idiots are always with us.

PS. If you think for a moment we made these up, think again!

*   *   *

And it didn't stop there. Their website also had a page dedicated to the *Hall of Shame.* This is where Cerretini re-posted negative *Yelp* reviews and lashed out at the reviewers. These weren't anonymous attacks, like the *Village Idiot* page. Reviewers' *Yelp* usernames were included along with their comments. The first review was from the CEO of *Yelp.*

*   *   *

Jeremy "Big Papa" S., San Francisco, California

In 2005, *Yelp's* CEO Jeremy Stoppleman walked into one of our restaurants, bringing along his God complex and his gang of *Yelp* Elite. His majesty obviously expected some sort of special treatment and obviously he wasn't going to get it from us. We gave him an extra chair for his ego, of course, but that was as far as we would go. That same evening he posted a negative review for us on his site, *Yelp*.

Can you blame him? Of course not!

But, a few hours later his sales people started to call and harass us into buying ads on *Yelp* in order to "manage" our reviews and rating.

The idiot had no idea he had just walked into the wrong village. Only a one-of-a-kind genius would try to extort the Italians. Would you try to teach Michael Jordan to play basketball?

In honor of Jeremy, here are some of the real reviews and our real replies that we enjoyed thanks to *Yelp*. All of them have been hidden or deleted by *Yelp*, but not to worry, we got screenshots!

Mike M., Richmond, California

Went there tonight for maybe the fourth time. Every previous time was fine. This time, I went to the restroom to wash my hands. Had to use a key hitched to a spoon about a foot long to get in. The water didn't work, neither hot or cold. I told the woman behind the bar. She walked into the kitchen, then out again. After a little while I tried again. Same thing. No water. I tried both hot and cold settings again.

I'm reporting them to the health department because the water didn't work, and I wasn't sure employees were washing their hands after using the restroom. So the cook comes out, checks the water, and says 'it works.' I said 'show me.' So we walked into the restroom, and he pushed the knob down, and water came out.

It wasn't the type of faucet that usually requires that. It was an ordinary looking knob like you'd turn one way for hot, one way for cold. I'm 65. I've used many different types of faucets quite successfully.

Our Public Reply

You are ADORABLE!

We grew up in Italy and as little kids we were going to the circus to see the clowns. As adults we opened a restaurant in Richmond and guess what!? The clowns are coming here for dinner and the entertainment is free.

We think of you as a national treasure, as is *Mr. Bean* for the British. We can only imagine your face and frustration when you found yourself dealing with this strange device in the bathroom, a magic instrument, some new technology from another planet, or maybe an Italian faucet that has not been translated into English for you.

Doesn't matter if the hundreds of customers that use our restrooms weekly easily wash their hands, it's still a bad faucet, bad bad faucet, that does not like you.

Yes. You should contact immediately the proper departments and also the White House. The President needs to be informed about this mysterious device placed in our bathroom. We are so glad you did not hurt yourself trying to make the faucet work.

Next time the circus is in town please stop by again. We will take you to Home Depot and Bed Bath & Beyond so you can play all day with all these magic faucets.

Thank you funny man for making our evening less boring. We need to have some fun sometime. We are hoping that our faucet will become a local attraction and you become an inspiration for new young comedians. This one was to good to be true. We have to share with the public. Now you are in our Hall of Fame. Congratulations!

*   *   *

The finishing touch was a perfect illustration of Exposing.

Botto Bistro didn't hide their weirdness. They didn't hide their weaknesses. They proudly announced, in writing, what they couldn't and wouldn't do for their customers. They also told customers where they could get cheaper normal pizza with ranch dressing at the nearest Costco.

Photo Credit: Davide Cerretini

They also exposed their no-nonsense philosophy on the FAQ page of their website. There are so many gems that it was hard to pick just one.

* * *

Our FAQ page has been featured all over the world by all major media outlets. It has been up for 7 years and has been one of the major tools in our Anti-*Yelp* campaign and our Anti-Idiot customer screening.

Q. May I give you a suggestion?

A. This is a very tricky question. But frankly, the answer is 'no thanks'. We believe too much constructive criticism can be confusing. We truly believe in what we're doing and we are committed to giving our best, as we've done successfully for the last 20 years.

There are already many ways and places where you can express your culinary knowledge and restaurant business know-how, like *Yelp*. If and when we decide to ask a professional for suggestions we will contact a restaurant consultant and gladly pay for his time. In the meantime, it seems like we don't need it!

Remember that if we want to hear your opinion we will ask you for it, we are not shy.

* * *

Botto's flaws made them awesome. They succeeded by augmenting, combining almost all of the FLAWSOME strategies to build a truly remarkable restaurant.

Cerretini sold Botto Bistro to Mountain Mike's Pizza in early 2020. However, his attack on Yelp isn't over. He continues to maintain the Botto website in an effort to spread the word about his distaste for their business practices.

And what about *Yelp*? In September 2014, when they started a war with Botto Bistro, their stock was trading at $82.42 per share and their company was worth over $6 billion. As of this writing in early 2021, their stock is trading at $39.30 per share and the company is worth just $2.95 billion. Along the way, their stock dropped as low as $15.56 per share. In the end, Davide didn't kill Goliath, but he did cut the giant in half.

PERSONAL BRANDING PROFILE

Davide Cerretini is now *The One-Star Chef*. He didn't just augment at Botto Bistro. He kept it going by using Exposing in his personal branding. When you visit *1StarChef.com*, you can sign up for The One Star Cooking Club, enroll in cooking classes, or meet the *Most Infamous Chef on the Internet*.

Alt Hotels is another great example of augmenting. The Canadian hotel chain succeeds by "offering a unique alternative to conventional hotels." They practice Opposing by Withholding most of the services that their competitors provide, and then they created a campaign that Flaunts and Exposes all the things you won't find at their hotels. It's called "We Do Less."

Each of the five ads focuses on what they don't do and what they do instead. They are attracting the customers who want what they have and repelling, or Antagonizing, the customers who want what they don't have. We discussed this in the chapter on Alignment.

We **don't** have a mini bar.	We **do** have a hip lounge.
We **don't** have a concierge.	We **do** have an app with all the hot spots.
We **don't** have a pool.	We **do** have a pool table.
We **don't** offer room service.	We **do** have fresh grab-and-go meals.
We **don't** have a bellman.	We **do** have a versatile helpful staff.

Alt Hotels doesn't apologize for their flaws and they don't hide them. They expose them in their advertising. Each weakness is deliberately designed. They don't exceed expectations. They don't even meet expectations. They do less.

Alt Hotels succeeds by combining five of the eight FLAWSOME strategies. That's impressive, but there's another company that takes Augmenting to the next level.

Imagine a grocery store that practices an extreme version of Withholding. They don't advertise on television. They don't use social media. They don't put items on sale. They don't accept coupons. They don't have a loyalty card. They don't have a self-checkout. They don't advertise in the newspaper. They have narrow aisles and small parking lots. They don't offer online ordering or pickup. They have a small selection of items, about 90 percent less than most grocery stores.

Despite their success, they will not do an IPO. They are privately held, offer no public statements, and share none of their records. They do not gather customer data and they are "aggressively low-tech." They have only 500 stores, compared to 2,000 Krogers and 4,000 Walmarts. Additionally, all of this Withholding enables Trader Joe's to offer products that are 32 percent cheaper than Whole Foods.

It's hard to believe that a grocery store like that could be successful. It seems like they've gone too far already, but what if they augmented Withholding with some Lopsiding?

What if they hired more employees, while all of their competitors are trying to reduce staffing costs? What if they paid those employees twice as much as everyone else in the industry? What if they paid those employees to do things that no one else even does?

For example, they have employees directing traffic at the checkout line: one telling you which register to go to, one pulling you out of the big queue and into the final queue; and one or two holding up handmade signs marking the middle of the queue and the beginning. That's three or four employees to do the job that most stores use zero employees to do.[41]

In another unusual move, Trader Joe's does their stocking during the day, instead of the night. Their goal is to increase employee interactions with customers. This is in direct contradiction to most grocery stores, who are trying to minimize those interactions.

And they're not done. Now it's time to add in some Antagonizing. They don't sell any branded foods, only private labels. So you can't get the most common and popular foods that you're used to. This is going to make some people upset.

They offer mostly strange and uncommon foods. Some of their best sellers include: spatchcocked lemon-rosemary chicken, kohlrabi salad blend, sea salt & turbinado sugar chocolate almonds, and chicken tikka masala. This means that if you stop in on your way home and you're hoping to pick up some Kraft Macaroni & Cheese or General Mills' Honey Nut Cheerios, you'll be disappointed.

And even if you are a regular customer, they regularly eliminate foods that people enjoy in order to introduce new ones. "You might see your peach mango salsa disappear, but there'll be something new to try that you can offer at your next cocktail party and wow people with."

Finally, Traders Joe's is a master of Micro-Weirding.

The late Joseph Coulombe conceived an idea for a supermarket while vacationing in the Caribbean. He opened his first store in Pasadena in 1967. Coulombe noticed that as Americans began to

---

41. https://freakonomics.com/podcast/trader-joes-rebroadcast/

travel more, it was difficult to purchase the foreign foods and wines they enjoyed while traveling once they returned home. His name and a South Seas motif became the inspiration for Trader Joe's.

Beyond the staff wearing Caribbean shirts, when it comes to embracing weirdness and providing a good customer service experience, Trader Joe's understands the importance of taking care of the customer. While the customer base itself is not made up of children, it is made up of many people who have children. Trader Joe's has not ignored that—in fact, they've embraced it since their founding. In addition to offering a variety of free samples, they also have a stuffed whale and miniature shopping carts. As for the stuffed whale, if you find it, your child gets a treat out of a treasure box and then you get to hide the whale yourself for others to find.

Trader Joe's customers love them in weird and wonderful ways. They have raving fans like Kirk Desermia, who lives in Alaska and doesn't have a Trader Joe's within 2,000 miles. So he finds them every time he travels and fills at least one suitcase with his favorite foods and some new one as well. When he returns from his trips, he shares what he brings back with his neighbors and friends in the hopes of turning them into fans. He also started a *Facebook* page to get a Trader Joe's store in Alaska and sends regular emails to the company. As you might have guessed, he has never received a reply from Trader Joe's.

Trader Joe's exceptionally unusual combination of strategies is working. They have better sales per square foot ($2,000) than any other grocery store, beating Walmart ($600) by more than 300 percent and Whole Foods ($1,200) by 65 percent.

And remember all of those extra employees? Trader Joe's is regularly ranked as one of the 100 Best Companies to Work for in America by *Fortune*.

Our next example is a low-cost airline. You've probably been waiting for this. You knew that, sooner or later, we had to profile Southwest Airlines, but that's not the airline we want to talk about.

Spirit Airlines actually began as a trucking company in Michigan in 1964. They started shipping via air in the 1970s, added passenger service in 1980, and changed their name to Spirit Airlines in 1992. In a world of low-cost airlines, they are an ultra-low-cost airline. They keep process low with a brutal combination of withholding and antagonizing.

Spirit pioneered an a la carte pricing model that includes a $3 charge for in-flight beverages and a $10 fee for printing a boarding pass at the service desk. Former CEO Ben Baldanza was proud of the fact that Spirit was the first airline to charge for a checked bag.

Spirit's restrictive policies and poor customer service have led to a tidal wave of complaints, but the company isn't apologizing or changing course. "Our complaints are statistically much higher," Baldanza admits, "but compared to the number of people traveling with us, it's a tiny drop in the ocean. We're the Walmart or the McDonald's—not the Nordstrom's—of the airline industry," Baldanza says. "No one walks into McDonald's and gets disappointed when they don't see filet mignon on the menu."

Spirit withholds almost everything that customers expect, and only provides it for an additional fee. They also use sexual innuendo in their advertisements, which is Antagonizing to many customers.

Embracing innuendo and being controversial have become hallmarks of Spirit Airlines. They are known for loud ad campaigns with sexual innuendo, ads in passenger cabins, and even ads on flight attendants' aprons. Here are some recent advertisements with references to wieners, MILFs, and balls.

Spirit Airlines does an amazing job of combining FLAWSOME strategies, but no one Augments better than this next company.

To this point, we haven't talked about Southwest Airlines. That was deliberate. Everyone talks about Southwest Airlines. They are probably the most well-known and most successful example of differentiation in American business. We didn't want to waste your time by telling you what you already know and sharing examples you've already heard.

But we came up with a way to capitalize on Southwest's fame. We want to give you a chance to test your FLAWSOME knowledge with a short quiz. We'll tell you what Southwest does differently and you fill in the blank with the corresponding strategy. Sometimes more than one strategy might fit.

Here's a sample. . . Southwest doesn't provide in-flight meals.

This is an example of <u>Withholding</u>.

Here's your quiz:

Question #1. Southwest is unapologetic about it's cheap no-frills flights.

This is an example of? _____

Question #2. Southwest Airlines is built on love. Their base is at Dallas Love Field. There is a heart in their logo. There is also a heart on the belly of each one of their planes. "It's the finishing touch that makes the Southwest brand unique, demonstrating that Southwest cares about each and every customer. Even on the belly of the plane, the heart is a symbolic reminder that we put our hearts into every flight."

Southwest hires staff based specifically on their friendliness and empathy. They pride themselves on their customer service.

This is an example of? _____

Question #3. After a customer consistently sent complaints about Southwest's failure to provide first class, in-flight meals, assigned seating, and just about everything else, Herb Kelleher, the founder and CEO, sent her a letter that said simply, "We will miss you. Love, Herb."

This is an example of? _____

Question #4. Southwest doesn't have first class. They don't have assigned seating. They only sell tickets on their website or app. They don't have airport lounges. You can't fly Southwest to Europe, Asia, Africa, Australia, or South America. They have no partner airlines.

This is an example of? _____

Question #5. Most airlines fly an entire fleet of planes. From the small Embraer E170 regional jet (that David famously struggles to go to the bathroom in) to the monstrous Airbus 380 that can accommodate over 800 passengers. Most airlines buy planes from multiple manufacturers. By contrast, Southwest only has one type of plane from one manufacturer. They exclusively fly the Boeing 737. They have 747 . . . 737s to be exact.

This is an example of _____

Question #6. Southwest flies point to point. They don't have hub and spoke routes like the other airlines. Southwest also flies into and out of smaller secondary airports, instead of the large major airports used by most other carriers.

- Dallas Love Field, instead of Dallas Fort Worth International
- Chicago Midway, instead of Chicago O'Hare International
- Houston Hobby, instead of Houston George Bush Intercontinental

This is an example of? _____

Question #7. Southwest flight attendants often will often create their own version of the flight safety announcement, changing the boring lingo into a rap or comedy routine.

In their book, *The Power of Moments*, Chip and Dan Heath share a story about visiting Southwest Airlines headquarters. They asked the team if they knew the impact of these silly improvisations. The team said they didn't, but they did have the data to figure it out.

It turns out that humorous safety announcements take place on only 1.5 percent of all Southwest flights. The data shows that passengers on those flights flew half a flight more the following year. That additional flying represents $138 million of revenue for Southwest. If they were able to increase that percentage from 1.5 to 3 percent, that would drive an additional $138 million of revenue for Southwest. Sometimes, little things can make a big difference.

This is an example of? _____

Question #8. Transfarency. Southwest makes clear and simple what others make complex and murky. Southwest doesn't charge fees like other airlines. Not only do "Bags Fly Free," there are no change or cancellation fees when you fly Southwest.

This is an example of? _____

Question #9. Southwest succeeds by finding customers who want what they offer and don't want what Southwest doesn't offer.

This is an example of? _____

Question #10. Southwest was unusual from the very beginning when they were founded in 1967. They've gotten even more unique over the last 55 years.

This is an example of? _____

Question #11. Southwest combines multiple FLAWSOME strategies together to create an incredibly differentiated business.

This is an example of? _____

Question 12. Southwest uses FLAWSOME strategies to defeat larger competitors.

This is an example of? _____

Answer Key

1. Flaunting

2. Lopsiding

3. Antagonizing

4. Withholding

5. Swerving

6. Opposing

7. Micro-Weirding

8. Exposing

9. Alignment

10. Amplifying

11. Augmenting

12. Attacking

Augmenting works. Augmenting pays off. Augmenting is effective.

Southwest is the most profitable airline in the United States and one of the most profitable companies of any kind in the country. At one point, they set the record for consecutive profitable quarters by staying in the black for more than thirty years. They were ranked #3 on *Indeed's* list of Top-Rated Workplaces and were *J.D. Power's* highest ranked low-cost carrier for customer satisfaction for three years in a row.

The final chapter is about Attacking the competition by identifying the weakness in their obviously powerful strength and then deploying the strength that is hiding inside of your apparent weakness.

CHAPTER 20

ATTACK

*"Of supreme importance in war
is to attack the enemy's strategy."*

— Sun Tzu

In the movie *Enemy of the State*, a conspiracy-theory thriller, Gene Hackman tries to help Will Smith evade government agents who are trying to capture him. Smith sees his situation as hopeless, but Hackman changes his perspective by offering a lesson in guerrilla warfare.

"You use your weakness as strength. They're big and you're small. But that means they're slow and you're fast. They're exposed and you're hidden." He reframes the enemy's apparent strength (being big) as weakness (slow and exposed) and Smith's apparent weakness (being small) as strength (fast and hidden).

This is the essence of attacking, identifying the weaknesses in your enemy's obvious strengths and fighting them with the strengths that are hiding in your apparent weaknesses.

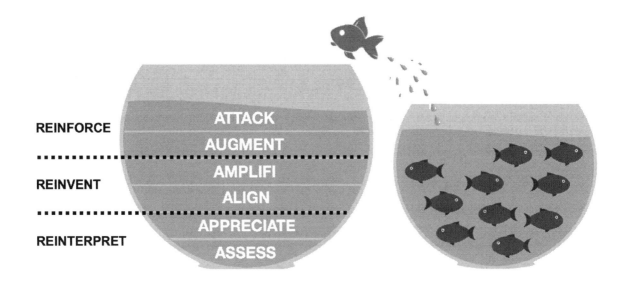

That might seem complicated or confusing or ineffective, so let's look at some real world examples.

Nothing vs. Everything

Google is a great organizational example of attacking. *Yahoo* was the search engine leader before *Google* became the dominant force that it is today. So how did *Google* win? There are a lot of answers to that question, but one is particularly useful for our purposes.

Look at *Yahoo!'s* homepage. The first thing you probably notice is how full it is. There are innumerable links, stories, and banners. There's news, weather, sports, and more. Everything you need, and a lot you probably don't need, is right there.

Now, look at *Google's* homepage. The first thing you notice is how empty it is. There is just a search box. Nothing you need is right there, so you'll have to search for it.

Google didn't try to beat *Yahoo!* by finding a way to put even more information, links, and advertisements on their homepage. Instead, *Google* practiced minimizing. They did less, not more.

Google's approach framed all of *Yahoo!'s* strengths as weaknesses. *Yahoo!* wasn't informative. It was cluttered. *Yahoo!* wasn't helpful. It was confusing. *Yahoo!* was controlling. They told you what to read instead of helping you find what you wanted.

In contrast, *Google* wasn't cluttered. It was clean and neat. *Google* wasn't confusing. It was simple. *Google* wasn't telling you where to go. It was there to help you find what you wanted.

Google dramatically underperformed compared to *Yahoo!'s* ability to put everything in one place, but this allowed them to over-deliver on what many customers wanted, which was a faster and more relevant search.

Google's attack worked spectacularly. Their name has become synonymous with search and they've become one of the most powerful companies in the world. They have a market cap of more than $1.5 trillion and profits of $40.2 billion in 2020. *Google's* employees regularly rank them as one of the best places to work.

Now vs. Later

The online dating company *eHarmony* uses extremely detailed profiles and matching software to help people find their soul mate. Users are asked to provide extensive information about themselves in order to connect them with a perfect match. Their advertisements feature Dr. Neal Clark Warren and they claim to have created more marriages than any other service. This strategy has been profitable and has earned them many awards. The Online Dating Industry named them the Most Innovative Company in 2016. The iDate Awards recognized them as the Best Dating Site in 2018 and 2020. They are doctors and scientists and experts and they help people find "the one" forever. How can you compete with that?

The obvious and most common approach would be to build a competing company with better matching algorithms and smarter scientists analyzing more personal information in order to create even more lifetime relationships than *eHarmony*. But that strategy would be difficult and costly and would likely end in failure.

A better approach would be to challenge the entire foundation of *eHarmony's* strategy. Instead of helping people find "the one" forever, just help them find anyone for right now.

That is what *Tinder* did. They provide simple profile photos, instead of detailed personal information. They don't have any algorithms or relationship experts. They let users choose their own match. They don't help people find lasting love. Finding Mr. or Mrs. Right takes time and energy. Tinder helps people hook up with someone tonight.

Both *eHarmony* and *Tinder* are successful companies, but they have opposite goals and tactics. It's not that one is succeeding and the other is failing. They are both effectively accomplishing different goals for different customers. Attacking by doing the opposite of the market leader doesn't mean that what you are opposing is bad, ineffective, or unsuccessful. Furthermore, as successful as *Tinder* is, they can still be attacked.

Girls vs. Boys

Bumble is similar to *Tinder*, but attacks them by Withholding. Men can't initiate matches. Former *Tinder* VP of Marketing, Whitney Wolfe Herd, created *Bumble* in 2014 by opposing previous dating norms, "There's only one significant thing that separates *Bumble* from *Tinder*. On *Bumble*, girls hold all the power." The app puts women in charge. Only they can initiate a conversation with a match, and if it doesn't happen within 24 hours, the match expires.

Is it working? Yes. Whitney shared, "Everyone in the dating business wants to know what women want - it's the billion-dollar question... But it's simple: put one in charge, and you find out."

The *Bumble* IPO made the Wolfe Herd the youngest self-made billionaire at age 31. She is currently worth an estimated $1.3 billion dollars.

Fleeting vs. Forever

"The internet is forever." You've probably heard some version of this statement before. It means that once your personal information or a tweet or a photo or an article is on the internet, it will never disappear. There is no reliable way to remove it. *Facebook* even has a legacy option so that your profile can be maintained by someone else after your death.

For years, this permanence was seen as a very positive feature. The internet was the perfect place to preserve things that might otherwise be lost. It was the perfect place for photographs.

Shutterfly was founded in 1999 as a way for people to store and share their photos online. *Flickr* started in 2004 with a similar mission. *Instagram* followed in 2010 and quickly became the dominant player in photo sharing.

Here we go again. How do you compete with that? Companies with decades of experience. Others with cool cutting-edge features.

The most common and obvious path is to try to do what your competitors are doing, but do it even better. Better sharing. Better storage. Better features. Beat them at their own game. But as you've probably guessed, there's another way.

Just make the pictures disappear. That's right. Don't store them. Don't preserve them forever. Delete them by default. Make them fleeting, ephemeral.

That was Evan Spiegel's idea when he was in graduate school at Stanford University. He presented it to his class and got terribly negative feedback. Everyone told him it wouldn't work. Well, that's not completely true. A venture capitalist happened to be in the class during Spiegel's presentation. He thought the idea could work, but only if the pictures were permanent, instead of temporary, and if Spiegel agreed to partner with Best Buy.

In other words, his unconventional and counter-intuitive plan for a company would work, if he changed his plan to be the same as all of his competitors.

Fortunately, Spiegel didn't listen to the criticism and *Snapchat* debuted in 2011. Impermanence wasn't just one of their early features. It was the primary feature. The main difference between *Snapchat* and its competitors, at least at the beginning, was that the pictures being shared would automatically be deleted from the recipient's device.

We love Spiegel's explanation of the philosophy behind their decision. "*Snapchat* isn't about capturing the traditional Kodak moment. It's about communicating with the full range of human emotion - not just what appears to be pretty or perfect." He believed that the permanence of photos on other sites led to anxiety about what to post and created pressure for people to only post ideal or positive images. He thought that fleeting photos would free people to spend less time editing their appearance to make it conform to societal norms.

It is important to note at this point that further development of the app included filters which both distort and perfect people's faces and bodies.

Almost ten years after *Snapchat* was released, they have 229 million daily users creating more than four billion snaps per day and their market cap is over $78 billion. They attacked their competition by framing permanence as a weakness and impermanence as a strength. In doing so, they didn't just go against the conventions of their competitors. They went against the conventions of the Internet itself.

Along the way, they didn't just succeed. They changed the entire social media industry. All the major players now have a "stories" feature in which users can post photos and videos that will disappear after a predetermined period of time. *Facebook* does it. *Instagram* does it. Even *LinkedIn* does it. But *Snapchat* started it, and they did so at a time when it seemed ridiculous, outrageous, and foolish.

Primitive vs. Advanced

Video games are an arms race, both literally and figuratively. Companies use more and more advanced technology to create games that are incredibly realistic. In first-person shooter games, the players feel like they are in the middle of a real battle. Successful franchises like *Call of Duty* stay popular through constant improvements in technology, graphics, and gameplay. The goal of simulating real-life is so powerful that virtual reality and video games are merging into a completely immersive experience. To be clear, this formula works. Since 2003, *Call of Duty* has sold more than 300 million copies, making it the most successful video game franchise created in the United States, one of the highest grossing franchises ever, and the best-selling first person shooter game of all time.

So how do you compete with that? Imagine that you love video games and you love to create video games. How would you start your company? What kind of game would you create?

The tendency would be to emulate the success of existing games. Violence. Life-like simulation. Advanced technology. It would probably seem like a non-negotiable requirement to be right on the edge of what is possible with computing and communications. This isn't the wrong approach and there are companies that have been successful competing in this way. In fact, it's what most video game companies do. They believe that if they don't, they'll fall behind and become irrelevant. But there's another option that is also effective.

Markus Persson was a video game designer and a huge fan of video games. He started programming on a home computer when he was seven and was playing early video games when he was eight. At the age of 25, he worked for a video game maker and saw firsthand the constantly escalating battle for technological supremacy. But he loved older video games and didn't think he was the only one who felt that way.

Instead of trying to create something new and improved, he started building something old and familiar. He wanted to include the best aspects of early video games that had become obsolete due to advancements in technology. He didn't believe that newer was better. He didn't believe that all elements of older games were worthless simply because it was now possible to do more.

His game was simple and technologically primitive. It didn't push the boundaries of what was possible. It didn't require high processing speeds and special graphics cards. In fact, it is commonly described as blocky and rough, like everything was made of LEGOs. Unlike games such as *Call of Duty*, there were no specific goals, no levels of achievement, and no pre-designed worlds. You didn't play the game, as much as you built the game.

So did it work? Was this rudimentary and old-fashioned game able to compete? Absolutely. In fact, Persson's game didn't just compete. It dominated the world of video games.

The game that Persson created was *Minecraft*, and it became the best-selling video game of all-time with over 200 million copies sold and 126 million monthly active users. In 2014, just five years after it was created, *Minecraft* was sold to Microsoft for $2.5 billion.

This is a great example of attacking. *Minecraft* framed their competitor's strengths as weaknesses, and all of their own weaknesses as strengths.

Let's start with the competition.

Advanced video games are very expensive to create. This requires a lot of investment, in time, people, and money, and makes every game a big risk. If the game isn't successful, the company can go bankrupt. The stakes are very high, because the sales of the game have to at least cover the huge costs of creating it.

Primitive video games are inexpensive to create. This lowers the risk and makes it easier to experiment. If the game isn't successful, the company can simply create another game. The stakes are very low, because the costs of creating it were also low.

Little vs. Big

Amazon is big. Very, very big. They sell almost everything, to almost everyone, almost everywhere, every hour of every day.

How do you compete with that? Is it possible to be bigger than Amazon? Can you sell more things, to more people, in more places, more often? Probably not. So what can you do?

What if you sold one thing, to a small number of people, in one place, for just one day? Would that work? Yes. It would.

Matt Rutledge created *Woot!* and it went online in July 2004. The site was simple. *Woot.com* offered one item, in limited amounts, only to US residents, for just one day or until the item sold out. Their tagline was "One Day, One Deal."

The items weren't announced in advance. It was like an online garage sale. First come. First served. It created an urgency that no one would ever feel with *Amazon*.

Products could not be exchanged because most items sold out. This added an element of risk and excitement that *Amazon* doesn't have.

There was no customer support. Buyers were directed to the manufacturer's website for assistance. Customers had to be willing to make a trade-off in order to get a bargain.

There was no free shipping, especially since many of the items were bulky and expensive to transport. The low prices often offset the shipping costs.

Woot's unconventional strategy worked so well that *Amazon* bought *Woot* in 2010 for $110 million. *Amazon* was smart enough to realize that *Woot* was a legitimate competitor.

They saw the strengths in *Woot's* apparent weaknesses and added *Woot* in order to diversify their company.

PERSONAL BRANDING PROFILE

Jennifer is pretty. She has blond hair and blue eyes. She is relatively tall and thin, but with curves in all the right places. According to online sources, she is 5' 7" tall and weighs 121 pounds. Her measurements are 38-24-35. She is attractive according to all of the classic American standards of beauty. Because of her stunning good looks, she became a very successful model and her fame increased. It started with television shows and then movies.

Melissa is pretty. She has brown hair and green eyes. She is not thin and not very tall. According to online sources, she is 5' 2" tall and weighs 207 pounds. Her measurements are 43-38-45. She isn't considered attractive according to most of the classic American standards of beauty. No one offered to hire her as a model.

Jennifer and Melissa were cousins. Melissa was a little bit older. She was born two years before Jennifer. She had a front row seat to Jennifer's growing success. It would have been easy for her to be frustrated and jealous. She could have decided that Jennifer was lucky and she wasn't. Jennifer was hot and she was not. She could have compared herself to all of Jennifer's strengths, which would have highlighted her apparent weaknesses. But that's not what she did.

Melissa pursued success by a different route. She didn't try to be prettier and thinner and hotter than Jennifer. She didn't try to become a more famous model. She became a stand-up comedian. She was hilarious. She ended up on television because she was funny. Then she ended up in movies. Now she has a star on the Hollywood Walk of Fame.

You might have already figured out that we are talking about Jenny McCarthy and Melissa McCarthy. Jenny became famous in 1993 when she was featured in *Playboy* magazine. She starred in her own sitcom called *Jenny*, hosted her own talk show, *The Jenny McCarthy Show*, co-hosted *The View*, and is currently a judge on *The Masked Singer*. She's been in a few moderately successful movies, like *Scream 3* and *Santa Baby*, but hasn't become a bona fide movie star.

On the other hand, Melissa has become a superstar. In addition to her success as an actress and comedian, she is also a writer, producer, and fashion designer. Here is a short list of her many accomplishments:

- Two Primetime Emmy Awards
- Two Academy Award nominations
- Two Golden Globe Award nominations
- *Time's* most influential people in the world in 2016
- *The New York Times'* 25 Greatest Actors of the 21st Century

Continued...

Her movie and television credits include:

- *Gilmore Girls*
- *Mike & Molly*
- *Saturday Night Live*
- *Identity Thief*
- *Bridesmaids*
- *The Heat*
- *Spy*
- *The Boss*
- *Tammy*

In addition to all of that, she also produces films with her husband and has her own plus-sized clothing line, Melissa McCarthy Seven7.

The story of Jenny and Melissa is a great example of Attacking. It looked like Jenny had all of the advantages, all of the strengths. It seemed like Melissa had a lot of disadvantages and weaknesses. It wasn't likely that Melissa could ever even come close to being as famous and successful as Jenny. But she did more than just match Jenny's success, she eclipsed it. She achieved this by competing on her own terms, by playing a different game. She didn't try to be like Jenny, but better. She decided to be like Melissa, and it worked.

We've now covered the six As of creating a Pink Goldfish. We began with "Assess" to understand our respective strengths and weaknesses. We then spent time to "Appreciate" how each of our perceived weaknesses have corresponding strengths. The "Align" step asks us to take an inventory of how we are coming across. Does our website, workplace, and marketing match up with our uniqueness? In "Amplifi" we explored the concepts of maximizing and minimizing. How can we turn up the dial in some areas or throttle down in others? Next, we looked at "Augment" to understand how we could leverage multiple strategies in the FLAWSOME framework. And now we've examined "Attack" to find ways to compete against the market leaders.

Now, let's examine the five biggest takeaways from *P!NK GOLDF!SH 2.0.*

CLOSING

CHAPTER 21

TOP FIVE TAKEAWAYS

"Don't try to stand out from the crowd...
Avoid crowds altogether."

— Hugh MacLeod

HERE ARE THE TOP FIVE TAKEAWAYS FROM *P!NK GOLDF!SH 2.0*:

1. IMPERFECTION WORKS

It's easy to follow the crowd. It's easy to blend in. It seems smart to do what other brands are doing. It feels safe. But it's not. Successful brands stick out. They are different. They are unusual. Every weakness has a corresponding strength.

2. THERE ARE MANY DIFFERENT WAYS TO BE DIFFERENT

We provided a lot of examples in this book, but we don't recommend that you imitate those examples. In the words of author and speaker Joseph Jaffe, "Once is witty, twice is shitty." We want you to see that there are an infinite number of ways to be unique. You can learn the principle from other brands, but you have to practice it in your own way. Who can you antagonize? How can you do the opposite? What can you withhold?

3. BE UNAPOLOGETIC

Be proud of what your brand does and what it doesn't do. Be proud of your brand's strengths and weaknesses. Don't apologize for your flaws and don't try to fix them. Instead, exploit your brand's imperfections.

4. TO PLEASE SOME CUSTOMERS, YOU HAVE TO DISPLEASE OTHERS

You can't be good at everything. You can't make everyone happy. So don't try. In fact, we think you should go out of your way to make some people unhappy. Choose whom you will reject. Decide whom to repel. Do it deliberately.

5. START SMALL—START NOW

You don't have to change your entire strategy all at once. You don't have to turn around completely, just swerve to the left or right. Look for a way to be micro-weird. Little things have a big impact (remember lagniappe). Don't wait. Deviate.

Here's how you can help us create more Pink Goldfish:

- apply what you've learned in this book to your brand
- share the book with others
- bring us in to speak at your conference
- book us for a workshop or session
- hire us to host a Goldfish Tank team-building, innovation experience
- connect with us on *LinkedIn*

ABOUT THE AUTHORS

WEIRD THINGS ABOUT STAN:

First thing he does when visiting a new country is to eat at McDonald's.

Favorite McDonald's was in India because he got to order a McTikka.

Stan is not related to Michael Phelps, but he has webbed toes and is banned from Olympic swimming.

Is obsessed with acronyms and bar tricks.

Has never broken a bone.

Has two teenage sons and a male cat.

Met his wife at baggage claim in the Amsterdam airport.

Is infamous for doing a weird flaming shot called the "Statue of Liberty."

Is famous for coining the first rule of advertising, "Never let the truth get in the way of a good story."

He struggles to think of weird things about himself.

Stan doesn't shake hands, but he will give you a fist bump.

WEIRD THINGS ABOUT DAVID:

He is 6'6" tall...6'9" in heels. His wife is just 5'3."

He has three daughters. He is the only man at his house. Even his dog is a girl.

He was once hit by a truck while running.

He has two screws in his elbow and two screws in his tibia.

He has been in the emergency room 11 times, once in the Ukraine.

He has eaten brains in Pakistan, barracuda in Nigeria, and eel in Chile.

His thumb looks like a big toe.

He has Morton's Toe. His second toe is longer than his big toe.

He is not good at lying.

He has not met any women at the baggage claim in Amsterdam.

He loves McDonald's shamrock shakes.

STAN PHELPS

Stan Phelps CSP (Certified Speaking Professional) is a best-selling author, keynote speaker, and workshop facilitator. He believes that today's organizations must focus on a meaningful differentiated experience (DX) to win the hearts of both employees and customers.

He is the founder of *StanPhelpsSpeaks.com* where he offers keynotes, workshops, and Goldfish Tank programs that are focused on driving loyalty and sales. The group helps organizations connect with the hearts and minds of customers and employees.

Prior to PurpleGoldfish.com, Stan had a 20-year career in marketing that included leadership positions at IMG, adidas, PGA Exhibitions, and Synergy. At Synergy, he worked on award-winning experiential programs for top brands such as KFC, Wachovia, NASCAR, Starbucks, and M&M's.

Stan is a TEDx speaker, a *Forbes* contributor, and IBM Futurist. His writing is syndicated on top sites such as *Customer Think* and *Business2Community.* He has spoken at more than 500 events in Australia, Bahrain, Canada, Ecuador, France, Germany, Holland, Israel, Japan, Malaysia, Peru, Russia, Singapore, Spain, Sweden, UK, and the US.

He is the author of the Goldfish Series of books:

- *Purple Goldfish*
- *Green Goldfish*
- *Golden Goldfish*
- *Blue Goldfish*

- *Purple Goldfish Service Edition*
- *Red Goldfish*
- *Pink Goldfish*
- *Yellow Goldfish*
- *Purple Goldfish Franchise Edition*
- *Gray Goldfish*
- *Green Goldfish 2.0*
- *Red Goldfish Nonprofit Edition*
- *Purple Goldfish 2.0*
- *Diamond Goldfish*
- *Silver Goldfish*
- *Red Goldfish Promo Edition*

He is also the author of *Bar Tricks, Bad Jokes, and Even Worse Stories.*

Stan received a BS in Marketing and Human Resources from Marist College, a JD/MBA from Villanova University, and a certificate for Achieving Breakthrough Service from Harvard Business School. He is a Certified Net Promoter Associate and has taught as an adjunct professor at NYU, Rutgers University, and Manhattanville College. Stan lives in Cary, North Carolina, with his wife, Jennifer, and two boys, Thomas & James.

To book Stan for an upcoming in-person or virtual keynote or workshop, go *stanphelpsspeaks.com.* You can reach Stan at stan@purplegoldfish.com or call +1.919.360.4702.

DAVID RENDALL

During the last fifteen years, David Rendall CSP has spoken to audiences on every inhabited continent. His clients include the US Air Force, Australian Government, and Fortune 50 companies such as Microsoft, AT&T, UnitedHealth Group, Fannie Mae, and State Farm.

Prior to becoming a Certified Speaking Professional, he was a leadership professor and stand-up comedian. He also managed nonprofit enterprises that provided employment for people with disabilities.

In between presentations, David competes in ultramarathons and Ironman triathlons.

David has a doctor of management degree in organizational leadership as well as a graduate degree in psychology. He is the author of four other books:

- *The Four Factors of Effective Leadership*
- *The Freak Factor*
- *The Freak Factor for Kids*
- *21st Century Leadership in the Arab World*

To book David for an upcoming in-person or virtual keynote or workshop, go to drendall.com. You can reach David at dave@drendall.com or call +1.919.222.6295.

GOLDFISH TANK PROGRAMS

Does your brand stand out in a crowded marketplace?

Does your team have the skillset to create innovative experiences?

Do you need a fun team-building experience that spurs creativity?

Consider GOLDFISH TANK, a fun way to build experience design capability and spark new ideas. The three-part in-person or virtual program can be done as a full-day, two half-days, or three 2-hour segments.

Here's an overview of the three parts:

1. Part One: LEARN CONCEPTS. This keynote style session uncovers the key concepts. We share a framework to expand thinking and challenge norms.

2. Part Two: TEAMWORK. This is a facilitated workshop session where we provide the space and clear criteria for team members to generate innovative ideas.

3. Part Three: PITCH CONTEST. Here we create a rapid-feedback construct. Using gamification, the teams compete by pitching their ideas.

ADDITIONAL INSPIRATION AND RECOMMENDED READING

- *Different, Youngme Moon*
- *Blue Ocean Strategy, W. Chan Kim and Renee Mauborgne*
- *Blue Ocean Shift, W. Chan Kim and Renee Mauborgne*
- *Purple Cow, Seth Godin*
- *The Freak Factor, David Rendall*
- *The Power of Moments, Chip and Dan Heath*
- *Made to Stick, Chip and Dan Heath*
- *Stand Out, Dorie Clark*
- *Barking Up the Wrong Tree, Eric Barker*
- *The Power of Small, Robert Koval and Linda Kaplan Thaler*
- *Free the Idea Monkey, Mike Maddock*
- *Uncommon Service, Frances Frei and Anne Morriss*
- *The Gifts of Imperfection, Brené Brown*
- *Becoming a Category of One, Joe Calloway*
- *Contagious, Jonah Berger*
- *Youtility, Jay Baer*
- *Small Giants, Bo Burlingham*
- *Talk Triggers, Jay Baer and Daniel Lemin*
- *Fascinate, Sally Hogshead*
- *Zag, Marty Neumeier*
- *The End of Average, Todd Rose*
- *Originals, Adam Grant*
- *David and Goliath, Malcolm Gladwell*
- *The Outsiders, William N. Thorndike Jr.*
- *America's Obsessives, Joshua Kendall*
- *Awkward, Ty Tashiro*
- *The Perfectionists, Simon Winchester*
- *Messy, Tim Harford*
- *Change to Strange, Daniel M. Cable*
- *Alchemy, Rory Sutherland*
- *Purple Goldfish 2.0, Stan Phelps & Evan Carroll*

OTHER COLORS IN THE GOLDFISH SERIES

After collecting over 1,001 examples and writing *Purple Goldfish*, Stan's thinking was slightly altered. He found that the companies who did the little extras for customers also applied the same principles for their employees. In fact, many of those successful companies seemed to place a greater emphasis on culture and putting their employees first to create competitive differentiation.

It led him to crowdsource another thousand examples. These examples were focused on the little things for employees to help drive engagement and reinforce culture. The result was the second book, *Green Goldfish*.

His outlook after *Green Goldfish* evolved once again. He had previously held the view that you should treat all your customers and all your employees the same. Stan came to realize that for most companies, 80 percent of profitability is created by just 20 percent of customers. In addition, 80 percent of the value that is created by a business comes from just 20 percent of the employees. You should not treat everyone the same; you should treat everyone fairly. The third book in the original trilogy became *Golden Goldfish*. Gold focuses on the little things you do for your "*vital few*" customers and employees in business.

The fourth book in the Goldfish series is *Blue Goldfish*, co-authored with Evan Carroll. Blue focuses on how to leverage technology, data, and analytics to create both prophets and profits. It examines the 3R's of relationship, responsiveness, and readiness. It was followed by *Red Goldfish*, co-authored with Graeme Newell. *Red Goldfish* examines how purpose is becoming the ultimate differentiator in business. It explores how business is evolving, the importance of putting purpose first, how to define your purpose, the eight purpose archetypes, and how to create the little things that bring purpose to life. *Pink Goldfish* was the sixth in the series and has subsequently been followed by *Yellow Goldfish* (Happiness), *Gray Goldfish* (Generational Insights), *Diamond Goldfish* (Sales/Client Management), and *Silver Goldfish* (Communication).

Here is a breakdown of the series:

Purple Goldfish 2.0 – 10 Ways to Attract Raving Customers. This book is based on the Purple Goldfish Project, a crowdsourcing effort that collected more than 1,001 examples of signature added value. Purple draws inspiration from the concept of lagniappe, providing 10 practical strategies for winning the hearts of customers and influencing positive word of mouth.

Green Goldfish 2.0 – Beyond Dollars: 15 Ways to Drive Employee Engagement and Reinforce Culture. *Green Goldfish* examines the importance of employee engagement in today's workplace. The book showcases 15 signature ways to increase employee engagement beyond compensation to reinforce the culture of an organization.

Golden Goldfish – The Vital Few: All Customers and Employees Are Not Created Equal. *Golden Goldfish* examines the importance of your top 20 percent of customers and employees. The book showcases nine ways to drive loyalty and retention with these two critical groups.

Blue Goldfish - Using Technology, Data, and Analytics to Drive Both Profits and Prophets. *Blue Goldfish* examines how to leverage technology, data, and analytics to do a "little something extra" to improve the experience for the customer. The book is based on a collection of over 300 case studies. It examines the three R's: Relationship, Responsiveness, and Readiness. *Blue Goldfish* also uncovers eight different ways to turn insights into action.

Red Goldfish - Motivating Sales and Loyalty Through Shared Passion and Purpose. Purpose is changing the way we work and how customers choose business partners. It is driving loyalty, and it's on its way to becoming the ultimate differentiator in business. *Red Goldfish* shares cutting edge examples and reveals the eight ways businesses can embrace purpose that drives employee engagement, fuels the bottom line, and makes an impact on the lives of those it serves.

Purple Goldfish Service Edition - 12 Ways Hotels, Restaurants, and Airlines Win the Right Customers. *Purple Goldfish Service Edition* is about differentiation via added value. Marketing to your existing customers via G.L.U.E. (giving little unexpected extras). Packed with over 100 examples, the book focuses on the 12 ways to do the "little extras" to improve the customer experience for restaurants, hotels, and airlines. The end result is increased sales, happier customers, and positive word of mouth.

Purple Goldfish Franchise Edition - The Ultimate S.Y.S.T.E.M. for Franchisors and Franchisees. Packed with over 100 best-practice examples, *Purple Goldfish Franchise Edition* focuses on the six keys to creating a successful franchise S.Y.S.T.E.M. and a dozen ways to create a signature customer experience.

Yellow Goldfish - Nine Ways to Drive Happiness in Business for Growth, Productivity, and Prosperity. There should only be one success metric in business and that's happiness. A Yellow Goldfish is any time a business does a little extra to contribute to the happiness of its customers, employees, or society. Based on nearly 300 case studies, *Yellow Goldfish* provides a nine-part framework for happiness-driven growth, productivity, and prosperity in business.

Gray Goldfish - Navigating the Gray Areas to Successfully Lead Every Generation. How do you successfully lead the five generations in today's workforce? You need tools to navigate. Filled with over 100 case studies and the Generational Matrix, *Gray Goldfish* provides the definitive map for leaders to follow as they recruit, train, manage, and inspire across the generations.

Red Goldfish Nonprofit Edition. The competition is fierce in the nonprofit world, even when competing in different spaces. This book explores the signature ways nonprofits reinforce their purpose and stand out in a crowded marketplace, whether it is an extra level of recognition for key donors, a special incentive designed to keep their best employees, or something simple like a luncheon to recognize volunteers or highest fundraisers. If you work at a nonprofit, this book will help you deliver "a little extra" to your stakeholders.

Diamond Goldfish - Excel Under Pressure & Thrive in the Game of Business. *Diamond Goldfish* uncovers how business is a game. It's a guide for driving sales and deepening client relationships. Based on the Diamond Rule, over 150 case studies, and the science-backed framework of Market Force, the book provides perspective and tools for winning in sales and client management.

Silver Goldfish - Loud & Clear: The 10 Keys to Delivering Memorable Business Presentations. How do you avoid giving the typical boring corporate presentation? You need the tools and the approach to delivering memorable presentations. Filled with 64 tips, *Silver Goldfish* provides 10 keys and a six-step approach to coming across Loud & Clear when presenting.

Red Goldfish Promo Edition. How can Promotional Marketing be connected to supporting nonprofits, sustainable initiatives, and give people a stronger brand connection? *Red Goldfish Promo Edition* shares leading-edge case studies in the categories of give back, diversity & inclusion, environmental, experience, and transparency & trust.

INDUSTRY INDEX

Made in the USA
Columbia, SC
25 June 2021